END
OF THE ROAD

Political-Economic Catastrophe from Fiat, Debt, Inflation Targeting and Inequalities

Louis Holder

Contents

To my family, my wife Gail, especially our children and grandchildren, Louis Jr., Sean, Anton, Eric, and Sarah, and their spouses, Lana, Alexis & Briana. Indeed, to all the younger generations of Gen X, Y, Z, & Alpha. May their future World be free from the mismanagement of the political economy, described herein, that leads to conflict, polarization, unfairness, and despair.

PREFACE

FOR SOME TIME now, the author has been concerned about the macro- economic direction taken by the major economies in the World across North America, Europe, and Asia. He made these concerns public in 2016 with nine-part series titled *The Future Begins Now*, published in a local periodical in Guyana, where he resides, a series which reproduced with permission from the publishers in Section Notes. The effort continues with this book.

The author has a long career in the private sector, with significant experience in public-service projects.

He currently occupies the position of Chairman, *CEO* and Finance Director in agro-processing and renewable energy companies located in Guyana, South America. Prior to that, he consulted at the largest manufacturing firm in the country on financial matters and measures to prevent unsolicited and hostile acquisitions.

His experience includes senior-level roles in the provision of wireless high-speed satellite bandwidth to governmental, commercial, and industrial clients.

As a young graduate with an Economics-focused degree, he worked at a large New York electric and gas utility company. This position would necessarily focus on microeconomics and during his employ there, he introduced a relatively novel pricing concept at the time, Real Time Pricing. Real Time Pricing is the pricing of large industrial customers whose energy consumption could affect the integrity of the system, and which often did at peak periods having been given incorrect price signals which development would have been dated. Pricing based on costs computed the day before would be more accurate for these large users and therefore would induce a more efficient consumption response.

Although the primary aim of writing is to express an opinion that our political economy is on a destructive path having assumed a short-term focus to wealth creation at the cost of long-term destruction, it is written more as an accessible supplement to formal learning, and particularly suited to students or anyone learning about Geopolitics and Macroeconomics. Accordingly, the language is very straightforward for easy comprehension despite covering macroeconomic concepts and issues, and without the jargon that can be most baffling to the uninitiated. So economic snippets such as *"The employment function only differs from the aggregate supply function in that it is, in effect, its inverse function and is defined in terms of the wage-unit; the object of the employment function being to relate the amount of the effective demand, measured in terms of the wage-unit, directed to a given firm or industry or to industry as a whole with the amount of employment, the supply price of the output of which will compare to that amount of effective demand."* (John Maynard Keynes, *The General Theory of Employment, Interest and Money*), will not appear anywhere in its text.

The book acknowledges that there are serious headwinds ahead and proposes solutions worth considering.

Where we are now, half the planet is burning while the other half is under water. Half is parched and can't sustain life and the half that can is being misruled. Rebellions, revolts, and conflicts are taking place everywhere. The rich are travelling to space because they can afford it while there are children who will never know the taste of a nutritious meal. And even for those who were touched by exceptionalism, despair has mostly taken hold. There is nothing inspiring to behold. Look around you and you will sense that the zeitgeist is that the future is filled with strife and darkness if we do nothing to reverse what got us where we are now. The young among us deserve no less.

The approach here is to provide an overview of those who influenced our thinking on how an economy should be managed, how those views and theories evolved over time, what is still relevant today, what are the institutions in an economy affected by poor management, and what are the economic parameters used to bring this about. With this background, we should have a clear sense of whether an economy is heading in the right direction or not, what is responsible for the course it has taken, and if corrective action is needed, how to proceed. The course most countries are on have not shown consistency with the accepted theory, is being manipulated by special interests especially of politicians, and much to the detriment of the younger generations unless corrected.

This book raises the alarm, but as a learner's aid, injects awareness in future generations that the missteps of their elders should be avoided at all costs.

Chapters are written to be read separately, requiring some repetition, and therefore can be understood independent of what preceded them.

PART 1

END OF THE ROAD

I

INTRODUCTION: POLITICAL ECONOMY

ALTHOUGH SUMERIAN CUNEIFORM tablets ascribe the granting of Kingship by our Gods over six thousand years ago in Mesopotamia, the political economy we're focused on here is of a more recent vintage. It starts with Adam Smith in the 18th Century. Political economy is defined as the rules that a Country abides by and systems it supports in meeting operational and developmental goals of production, distribution, trade, and consumption for its social wellbeing.

Political economy or macroeconomics is underpinned by logic and observation, the latter allowing for the econometric modelling of the observable data. For example, a free market results in an efficient allocation of resources as consumers express a preference for what goods and services meet their wants and needs, in what quantities and at what prices, and suppliers provide these goods and services as long as they are adequately compensated for their efforts.

It's logical that if consumer needs/wants are being met at the cost of resources, these resources are not being used to produce extraneous goods and services and thus are being properly utilized. But there are rules based on this straightforward logic and observation. The market does not work as an efficient allocator of resources when market power exists, when there are restrictions to entry, and when it is not populated with several, or indeed many, participants.

Monopolies, monopsonies, and oligopolies existing within a market leads to lower efficiencies and well-regulated economies guard against such developments. In cases where monopolies are desirable from an environmental standpoint, such as utilities (to take advantage of the economies of scale offered up by the process, and to eliminate the unaesthetic view of multiple companies operating power lines down a residential street), regulation is necessary to remove their market power to control either supply or price. Unfortunately, even countries that refer to their economies as market, are hardly so with wage-floor and labor-cartel laws, duty restrictions on trade, and their failure to internalize social and environmental costs in prices.

But even when well regulated, a functioning market economy will not produce optimal social outcomes, outcomes compatible with our communal sense of fairness and economic justice.

In brief, the market allows the fittest to exist, like the jungle environment, and the weak fall by the wayside. However, humans no longer accept antiquated rules as part of their civilizations and therefore no society exists with a pure market economy. The appropriate body to make these adjustments is the government. After the market has made its allocations, governments have the obligation to step in and take corrective action to ensure everyone has the resources to meet its most basic needs, such as food and shelter, and conventional necessities.

INEQUALITY

Although the main contributing factors of inequality are anti-market from lack of proper regulation, such as rent seeking,[1] lack of opportunities, and garnering market power through the formation of monopolies, monopsonies and oligopolies, the market does provide more to some than to others from innovation, and superior skills and organization. The demand-supply interplay of the market can have serious implications on labor resources, lowering their compensations when surpluses exist. The market can peg wages so low that their recipients are unable to function in a normal society. As those with superior skills and fewer numerically can command more, those with less skills and numerically superior, must scrape by. The scourge of inequality.

As markets reward individuals for their innovations, productivity, and efficiency, those unable to compete at a high level are awarded a lesser share of production. The spread in these allocations can be enormous and billionaires are springing up like mushrooms in a wet, dark forest. The average worker has no means of getting even close although recent billion-dollar lotteries are making the exception.

And privately held corporations are not excepted. Peter Coy, a NYT Columnist, in a piece, "The Hidden Risk of Getting Paid in Stock Options", provided that around 10 years ago a privately held start-up company valued at $1 billion or more, referred to as a unicorn, was rare — in reality, nonexistent. But now, there are more than 650[2] of them in the United States.

Free markets, although efficient in their allocation of resources, create these disparities that must be addressed to avoid suffering and hardships.

---

1 Rent seeking is the "earning" of income with little or no change in production, unlike wages and profits, which are returns to productive labor and capital. The term is usually applied to the manipulation of public policy for gain, such as protections from competition and trade or just receipts of government subsidies. Rent seeking invariably results in inefficiencies and price increases".

2 https://www.cbinsights.com/research-unicorn-companies

Therefore, governments should be sized to not only meet the security and regulatory needs of their populations, but also to propose and administer transfer programs to make their societies fairer and reduce wealth inequality.

Political Economy can also be separated into its political and economic components. There are two components to each — democratic and command political structures, and market and centrally planned economies.

So, Political Economies fit into one of four combinations, with different degrees of modification. The USA and China both have similar economic components, seemingly largely driven by markets and competition, but totally different political systems. The *US* political system leans towards a democratic one whereas China has a command system. All systems have advantages and disadvantages. For example, whereas the American system allows more participation in decision making, the Chinese can turn them out more expeditiously, whether optimal or not.

The democratic/central planning model does not exist because, if given a choice, people, unless out of desperation, would not select an economic system with no history of success. The central-planning system, where decisions on production and distribution are made by a bureaucratic body instead of the market, has been tried in Eastern Europe and Asia and, in the long-term, it failed to improve the wellbeing of those relying on it.[3]

Except for North Korea, they were later abandoned. But have they really been discarded or have just taken a different approach to bypassing market solutions with similar consequences? This is explored further in this book.

---

3 Initially, in the Soviet Union, there was rapid growth during several of its 5-year central-planning periods in which it transformed from an agrarian society to superpower status. The transformation was so impressive to have influenced the ideological appeal in developing countries. But alas, the model was not sustainable and eventually central planning, as a developmental tool, succumbed to the market model as drastic competition from those economies took its toll.

Political Economies are dynamically evolving and changing. Before Adam Smith, the predominant Political Economy was Mercantilism, where nations believed that their social wellbeing/wealth was defined by the quantity of precious metals they possessed. They therefore tried to export more than they imported resulting in a positive balance of trade, built large shipping fleets as part of their export infrastructure, and even went to war to impose their exports on others. Britain's opium wars with China were intended to force China to continue buying its opium despite the detrimental effect it was having on its people. But that was not a concern for Britain. Its social wellbeing meant forcing opium into the bodies of the Chinese as this ensured the provision of the needed precious metals.

Happily, Adam Smith's "Invisible Hand" and David Ricardo's "Comparative Advantage" would thereafter have more influence in deciding the relationship between countries with respect to wealth and trade. The primary political economic index of a country's progress and welfare is the change in its real *Gross Domestic Product (GDP)*. *GDP* is the value of all goods and services produced in a country during a specific period and theoretically can be computed from production, expenditure, or income flows. The three approaches should provide identical estimates as all production generates incomes and expenditures equal to their values, that is, stuff must be paid for to be produced, and those payments are then spent to maintain households, investments by businesses and outlays by governments. In the real world, the three approaches do not always provide the same result leading to questions as to which approach is superior by allowing the lowest error rate.

THE PROBLEM WITH *GDP*

But *GDP*'s usefulness is not in its magnitude, but in its changes from one period to another. Such would indicate the magnitude of change

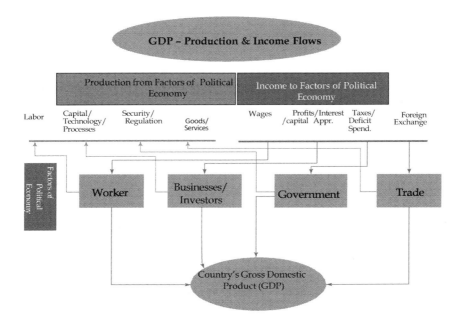

Figure 1

where increases are thought to be best for its population as the pie everyone shares is now larger. Decreases are resisted and are used as a narrow definition for a recession—negative growth in *GDP* for two successive quarters. Inflation is factored out to avoid misleading growth levels. **Figure 1** shows what comprises *GDP* and how it can be estimated by either summing up the total production of the country or its total income.

But some economists are starting to question the value and allure of the *GDP* index and with justification. Herman Daly, emeritus professor at the University of Maryland School of Public Policy, is the leading proponent of a steady-state economy, which New York Times correspondent David Marchese describes as *"one that forgoes the insatiable and environmentally destructive hunger for growth, recognizes the physical limitations of our planet and instead seeks a sustainable economic and ecological equilibrium"*.

In true Malthusian form, and after 50 years of study, Professor Daly questions whether growth, as currently measured, creates wealth or might it be increasing costs faster than benefits and is making us poorer? Growth invariably requires the consumption of resources, but no one is evaluating the effect of this consumption on economic and environmental factors. How much of what is claimed to be adding to growth and wealth is contributing to energy inflation and food insecurity, to climate change events, and to pandemics? However, to the extent that *GDP* growth offers advancement to poorer countries, Daly would expect that the wealthy countries make ecological room for the poor to catch up to an acceptable standard of living. In summary, *GDP* growth is likely doing us more harm than good, is inessential — one doesn't need to change cars every few years given their useful lives covering a couple of decades — but some leeway should be made to encourage growth in poorer countries to bring their standard of living to an acceptable level despite the degradation.

But politicians control the decision-making and as long as people feel better with growth and therefore likely to support the interests of the politicians, obsessing about it will not happen. Its consequences will be attributed to some other problems or kicked down the road for future generations to deal with.

DEBT AND CENTRAL INTERVENTIONS

Debt is encouraged for the same reason, it promotes growth. A popular public debt incurring tool among politicians is tax reductions without decreases in spending. Someone else's problem in the future as the current politician achieves goals of electability and addressing the needs of their lobbyists.

Some changes can be too complex to fully understand their ramifications for long term welfare and therefore evade the scrutiny of even those with free choice of their economic system.

For example, the monetarists, using financial tools—interest & inflation rates and money supply—to regulate the economy, are not relying on market-driven tools and as such are by no means different from the central-planners of the Soviet Union. Central Banks, the central planners in this case, set targets aimed at expanding/contracting the economy through the establishment of:

1. Short-term interest rates. These are man-made targets and which in turn affect interest rates of all other term loans in the economy. By setting short-term interest rates, the central planners usurp the market's prerogative to set interest rates based on savings levels,
2. Inflation targets with all the damaging effects these have on the value of the currency and future cost-of-living levels. But because inflation makes long term debt more affordable and thus doable, an amorphous level seems preferable to the central planners, and
3. Money supply. Through tools such as *Quantitative Easing*[4] and *Quantitative Tightening*[5], these central planners create money from nowhere and reduce its supply as corrective measures to their overaction.

These are man-made targets which could have, and do have, detrimental consequences on the economy. By adopting monetary central planning, the economies of America and Western Europe are no different from those where economic-central-planners were setting production and distribution goals and will face the similar destructive outcomes through market deviation.

---

4 *Quantitative easing (QE)* is a monetary policy where central banks encourage economic activity by buying a range of financial assets in the market.
5 *Quantitative tightening* is the action of removing liquidity, or money, from financial markets in order to cool down an overheating economy.

Further, the manipulation of the Political Economy of a country can also be accomplished by politicians for the sole purpose of their electability. When so done, it is never in the interest of society. Rules are undermined to gain or hold on to political power. To drive the growth in *GDP*, still seen as the leading index of wellbeing, they have been known to untether their currency from value-assets. Associated with this decoupling is the enormous appetite for debt, both private and public. In 2022, the total American debt to its *GDP* was 259%. Politicians, focused on *GDP*, are willing to have debt determine its rising level giving their constituents a false sense of improvement in their wellbeing, thus gaining a favorable job approval. But the cliff is ahead, and like with all such extravagances and interventions, their detrimental effects never fail to appear, leading to the destruction of economies and the associated displacement and social unrest that necessarily follow.

This book aims to explain why these interventions are damaging/destructive to an economy and what the new reset could look like. The reset would require the market, the most efficient allocator of resources, to operate unhindered, and to the extent that human outcomes are undesirable by such operation, for governments to step in and adjust, not to the market, but to the human condition. The evidence presented will be mainly from the US economy, but this would be representative of all similarly situated economies.

II

THE THEORISTS

MUCH HAS BEEN written about the men who advanced the concept of political economy worldwide. The objective here is to identify the main players whose contributions have led to and resulted in the evolution of the main political economic systems in effect today — democratic/market and command/market. There may be some controversy on the inclusion of Thomas Malthus in this listing, but it seems that ignoring or discrediting his main theory that *population growth will always tend to outrun the food supply and that betterment of humankind is impossible without strict limits on reproduction*, is a major factor in the decline of world economies. Malthus predicted that droughts, famine, pestilence, storms and conflicts, all negative impacts of climate change, will act to keep the world population in check when it creates disequilibrium from its unwarranted growth. As scientists now acknowledge the reality of climate change, Malthus' theory needs more focus in the minds of policymakers as measures for its abatement will not be effective without understanding its root cause.

This chapter identifies some important contributors to the function of political economy, summarizes their contributions, and briefly discusses how these have influenced what pertains today.

II (A) – ADAM SMITH

"He is in this (for his own gain), led by an invisible hand to promote an end which was no part of his intention."

Adam Smith

Adam Smith (1723–1790), A Scottish economist and the father of modern Political Economy, published a two-volume book in 1776, *An Inquiry into the Nature and Causes of the Wealth of Nations*, a revolutionary approach then to what constitutes wealth. Smith postulated that value comes from labor and the *Division of Labor*, where processes are broken up into several component-tasks to be performed by a worker of group of workers, contributes to lowering the cost of production, thereby increasing output and wealth. That is, the more one can produce with the same doses of labor and other inputs, the wealthier one becomes. Prior to Smith, wealth was the accumulation of precious metals acquired from other Nations through trade, a philosophy known as *Mercantilism*.

The beginning of the *Industrial Revolution* was a disruptive period for Britain as its craft labor was being displaced by larger and better capitalized operations. Attacks on equipment and processes were frequent. Smith basically supported the Industrialists whose operations separated processes into tasks which could be performed by individual or small groups of workers, unlike the craft industry which they were replacing. These separated tasks can then be performed by more specialized workers and done more routinely making for lower cost and increasing output. This is the recipe for nations becoming wealthy and a paradigm shift in the field of Political Economy.

Smith supported free labor markets unfettered by labor or employer unions but recognized and criticized the authorities for dealing with labor unions harshly while ignoring collaborations by employers. As labor unions would tend to force wages higher than market-determined levels, and employer collaborations the converse effect, the actions by the authorities would result in wages below the market of demand and supply. Despite the staunch support for the operation of free markets, Smith was not oblivious to the plight of the poor. He took note of the high children mortality of the Scottish-Highlands poor when he observed that it is not uncommon for a mother who bore twenty children to have two alive.

But it is thought that Smith's greatest and enduring contribution was his support for free markets as captured in his metaphor, *Invisible Hand*, the force that takes and converts all decisions made freely and in the interest of promoting and maximizing one's gain, into one that promotes and maximizes that of society. Smith was arguing against protectionism and government intervention in markets. The problem is that Smith assumed that there would be no barriers to the entry and exit of these markets, a necessary requirement for the *Invisible Hand* to work its magic. Today, monopolistic tendencies, market power, rent seeking, consolidations and acquisitions all work to defeat the power of the hand. Regulation by governments has become a necessity.

On debt, Smith, on equating the funding of wars with debt instead of taxes to prevent the populace from tiring and not supporting the effort, is prescient as to whether those debts would ever be repaid. The war in Vietnam is an excellent example of this position where the effort is funded by debt, never repaid and burdens future generations with its costs. Unfortunately, this applies to not just war debt but all public debt as it is almost never repaid by the generations that incurred it.

The free-market concept by Smith is probably the greatest contribution made by any in the field of political economy. It has been tried, with different degrees of freedom, in most countries and has proven to be more efficient and effective in creating wealth and wellbeing than the other approach, central planning. However, some tempering is required to a free-market system, referred to as *laissez faire*, to avoid dragging Homo Sapiens back into the jungle where survival of the fittest is the controlling operative.

II (B) – THOMAS ROBERT MALTHUS

"The power of population is indefinitely greater than the power in the earth to produce subsistence for man."

Thomas Malthus

Thomas Malthus (1766–1834) in his 1798 book, *An Essay on the Principle of Population*, advanced his position that *"Assuming then my postulate as granted, I say, that the power of population is indefinitely greater than the power in the Earth to produce subsistence for Man."* The postulate he refers to is that population, when unchecked, increases at a geometric ratio, whereas subsistence increases only in an arithmetical ratio. It was influenced by the growth rate of population in America at the time, which was estimated to have doubled over a 25-year period. So, in an example given, with a starting population of 7 million, it becomes 14 million in 25 years and 28 million in 50 years, but the food supply would only be able to sustain 21 million in 50 years. Thus, population growth, which he referred to as the superior power of population, cannot be checked without producing misery (hunger, pestilence, endemics, etc.) or vice (conflicts, crime, violence, and wars).

Malthus postulate above was obviously flawed and although he referred to *"dressing"* of the land, suggesting artificial intervention to increase output, he failed to recognize that such interventions would lead to sustenance being comparable to the *superior power of population*. As seen, all cases of development are characterized by the rapid decline of agricultural labor accompanied by increases in output from technological advances.

Whether his postulate was accurate or not, the importance of Malthus theory is in the natural curbs to unchecked population growth and which is very evident today. Over the past 50 years, the world population has doubled despite the efforts by China, until recently the most populous country, to limit its growth with a one-child-per-family policy. According to Worldometer, the world's population increased by 4.1 billion to 7.8 billion over the fifty years ending in 2020. The previous fifty years only saw an increase of 1.7 billion, forty percent of the 1970/2020 increase. The implication of this is enormous.

Malthus tied population expansion to increases in agricultural subsistence. As more food becomes available, he argued, couples marry earlier, children are healthier, and the population grows. In a modern society, the wealth effect, a feeling of a bright and optimistic future from rising unrealized assets values or income prospects, can be substituted for agricultural subsistence with the same impacts on population growth. And the English economist and philosopher, John Maynard Keynes agrees, ". . . the class who takes an active interest in their Stock Exchange investments, . . . are perhaps even more influenced in their readiness to spend by rises and falls in the value of their investments than the size of their incomes."[6]

The event over the past 50 years which contributed to this feeling of improved wellbeing was the introduction of *fiat* currency, where for some countries, the money supply can be increased seemingly unconstrained. This allowed rapid debt expansion, easy acquisition of goods and services, and an overall sense that future generations would always be improving their lot. Consequently, the population has more than doubled. One implication of Malthus theory, and perhaps the most important implication impacting the planet today, is when population exceeds the resources to sustain it, the planet self-corrects through *misery and vice*.

Accordingly, to avoid the *misery and* vice he predicted, Malthus was an early advocate of population control.

But in the 18th century, there weren't many options available as to how to achieve this. His prescription was to delay marriage. However today, there are so many more options for policymakers to adopt, but

---

6 Keynes, J.M., General Theory of Employment, Interest and Money, Calibre e-Books 0.8.63, December 13, 1935, p.218.

except for China, countries don't seem to recognize the problem associated with such a rapid population growth. The consequence of this failure and neglect to action is *misery and vice*, or in today's parlance, Climate Change.

Climate Change

Scientists tell us that the planet's climate is changing from man-made decisions and unless arrested, will lead to our destruction. These changes have led to droughts, famine, wildfires, floods, rising sea levels, pandemics and more, which all result in *misery*, and conflicts and wars, all part of *vice*, in Malthus' words. Still, our policymakers treat symptoms such as greenhouse gases and not the root problem, population growth. If the policy is to reduce greenhouse gasses by 10%, this would best be accomplished by reducing the population – birth rate less than death rate – by 10% to avoid self-correction through *misery and vice*.

II (C) – KARL MARX

"The history of all hitherto existing society is the history of class struggles."
Karl Marx & Friedrich Engels

Karl Marx's (1818–1883) theories, specifically that of Surplus Value, and which were laid out in his three-volume book *Das Kapital*, had more relevance in times where large pools of unskilled labor existed. This is mostly no longer the case with nations in the 21st Century.

According to Marx, surplus value is the value created by workers in excess of their wages, and which is appropriated by the capitalist as profit, when products are sold, or as capital when unsold. This then expands Adam Smith's hypothesis that all value comes from labor.

A logical extension of this view is that workers were not only entitled to their wages but also to profits as it was their efforts that produced both. The structure, therefore, that enabled workers to acquire both and thus be fully compensated for their labor, is worker cooperatives.

But Marx's contribution was a critique of *capitalism*. He didn't seem to have authorship in the establishment of a communist/socialist state or political economy, despite co-authoring *The Communist Manifesto* with collaborator Friedrich Engels. Engels was a German philosopher, who in 1848, besides co-authoring *The Communist Manifesto*, also edited the second and third volumes of *Das Kapital,* after Marx's death.

The Communist Manifesto summarizes Marx's and Engels' theories concerning the nature of society and politics and features their ideas for how the capitalist society of the time would eventually be replaced by *socialism*. According to Professor Richard D. Wolfe, a Marxian economist and professor emeritus of economics at the University of Massachusetts, Amherst, Communist political economic structure was not a product of Marx and by extension Engels, but the manifestation of his followers who sought to put his theory into political effect, followers like Lenin, Stalin, and Mao. *The Communist Manifesto* made recommendations some of which are more in line with measures later adopted by developed countries such as a progressive income tax system, abolition of child labor, and free public education. These recommendations anticipated the continuation of the capitalist system, in an adapted form.

As Marxism is a dead or dying philosophy, the only purpose for raising it here is that it gives the modern labor movement a rational foundation. By the early 20th Century, governments' intervention on behalf of labor was intentional and intended to stave off the movement in Western Countries towards *Communism*, which had taken hold in Eastern European and Asian Countries. By 1935, the American Government had passed the National Labor Relations Act which gave workers the right to organize into Unions. The intent was to give workers effective bargaining powers and to thwart the attractions of *Communism*.

However, the proportion of American workers in a Union has fallen off a cliff from a high of 34% in 1954 to 10.8% in 2020. Then, there were 14.3 million members in the U.S., down from 27.7 million in 1954. And union membership in the private sector, which is more elastic to automation and capital relocation, has fallen to 6.3%, one fifth that of public sector workers, at 34.8%. There is no longer the fear of workers' attraction to communist ideology, especially after the collapse of the Soviet Union in 1991.

The influence of Marx on the world's political economy is therefore on the wane despite attempts to revive labor-union representation, especially in the *US*, due to temporary labor shortages brought about by attrition/retirement during the *COVID* pandemic lockdowns. As a result, these attempts, which will increase the wage rate, will only serve to prolong the inflationary spiral, and increase the obsolescence of labor. Over the longer term, less-costly technology will increase the capital to labor ratio displacing the latter. Trade unions, along with labor-friendly legislation, are major restrictions to the labor market attaining sustainable full employment thereby quelling discontent and conflict.

Like other classical economists, such as Adam Smith and David Ricardo, the foundation for Marx theories were events of the times. These economists had seen labor producing all the value of society, as was certainly the case with the predominant industry of the times, the small family-run craft industry, and arrived at the conclusion of value, whether consumed or saved. But subsequent revolutions such as the industrial, electricity, digital, and now robotics and Artificial Intelligence, have introduced production factors never contemplated in their era of influence, and thus never given their proper significance. A mechanical crane used in construction is creating more value than labor if substituted, and thus properly employed, so are robots building cars and appliances in factories.

II (D) – JOHN MAYNARD KEYNES

"In the long run, we are all dead."

John Maynard Keynes

John Maynard Keynes (1883–1946) produced his magnum opus, *The General Theory of Employment, Interest and Money* in 1936 having been greatly influenced by the American depression of the 1930s. Therefore, the underpinnings of his works rests with ways to stimulate output during an economic downturn and to put workers back in employment. Keynes solution was for governments to engage in deficit spending, spending what they didn't have and couldn't raise through taxation.

Time Magazine in 1999 recognized how influential Keynes was when it identified him as one of the most important people of the century: *"His radical idea that governments should spend money they don't have may have saved capitalism."*

Many governments quickly followed Keynesian recommendations as it gave them an opportunity to increase spending at little political cost. But Keynes spoke of counter-cyclical public spending, a term implying that just as it is prudent to increase deficit spending to counter downturns, that it is also required to reduce government spending during upturns. The savings from these reductions, along with the additional tax revenues from the expansion, should be used to offset the debts incurred during the deficit spending. This would require discipline from politicians, so was never going to be practical. Consequently, the success of Keynesian economics was more a short-term phenomenon than a long-term one.

Keynesian economics was also at odds with that of the neoclassical which hold that the market, on its own, and in the long run, would make the necessary adjustments, especially to wages, to bring things back in balance. Keynes was not in agreement because of the so-called *wage stickiness*, where there are no barriers to increases but strong resistance to decreases. In any case, Keynes said that in the *"long-run, we are all dead,"* a reference that society should not have to wait an indeterminate period for automatic adjustments to have a desired impact.

Keynes also disagreed with classical thought on the value of money. Until he came along, money was not considered important to economics, the study of efficiently allocating society's resources. Keynes recognized the importance of money in a macroeconomic or political economy setting and opined *"But as soon as we pass to the problem of what determines output and employment as a whole, we require the complete theory of a Monetary Economy."*[7]

The Quantity Theory of Money he enunciated is not dissimilar to that of the Austrian School of Economics, which holds that with unemployment, increases in the money supply will work to increase the employment rate, but as the economy approaches full employment, increases in the money supply will result in the increase in inflation.

Monetarism

Keynes had his critics, one being Milton Friedman, with a monetarist bent, from the Chicago School of Economics.

Monetarism is the theory or practice of controlling the supply of money as the main means of stabilizing the economy.

Friedman argues that Keynesian policies could lead to both unemployment and inflation existing simultaneously, a phenomenon known as stagflation. And when stagflation occurred in the US in the early 1970s, Freidman was able to attribute it to the practice of Keynesian economics. As only the deficit spending of Keynesian Economics was ever practiced by policymakers, never the surplus reduction of debt, it seems patently unfair to blame Keynes for the condition.

---

7 Keynes, J.M., General Theory of Employment, Interest and Money, Calibre e-Books 0.8.63, December 13, 1935, p. 202.

Instead, Friedman has the new monetarism approach to peddle, and so whatever helped in discrediting alternatives was to be promoted. Today, the misapplication of Keynesian Economics and the Central Planning function of the Monetarists are clear contributors to the World's failing economies of major countries.

II (E) – DENG XIAOPING

"Black cat or white cat, if it can catch mice, it is a good cat."
Deng Xiaoping

Deng Xiaoping (1904–1997), who in 1978 inherited the management of the Chinese economy at its lowest ebb due to the Cultural Revolution, implemented remarkable reforms which reversed the fortunes of the Chinese from being one of the poorest nations on the face of the planet to now rising with the superpowers.

During this time, and according to a World Bank 2022 report, the number of poor in China fell by 770 million over the past 40 years. This is just astounding, and the architect of this astounding performance was Xiaoping.

Before Xiaoping, China's economy was a centrally planned one and was not performing. For comparison, another country with a large population, India, had a per capita income in 1978, under a market economy, of *US*$206. China's per capita income for the same year but with a centrally planned economy was *US*$156. By 2019, India's PCI had grown to *US*$2,101 whereas China's was *US*$10,144, a phenomenal performance. Xiaoping deserves much of the credit.

He followed through on the reforms known as the *Four Modernization* meant to address problems in agriculture, industry, science, and technology. Decision-making in agriculture was decentralized and peasant farmers were allowed to keep and sell excess farm produce at farm markets thereby increasing their incomes and thus motivation to increase output. Local municipalities and providences were allowed to invest in industries, and foreign investments encouraged moving industrial activities towards the export sector. The resulting foreign-exchange earnings generated investments in capital goods, driving advancements in technology and lowering production costs. The synergies gave China a major boost towards becoming the World manufacturer, which it still maintains today. Science and technology were addressed through a campaign to educate its students. These students, in large numbers, could be found on the campuses of the best tertiary educational institutions in the *US* and Europe. The *US* Embassy and *US* consulates in China reported that in 2020 to 2021, there were 317,000 Chinese students enrolled in *US* educational institutions and that China remains the top sender of students to the *US*. Chinese students have been travelling to the *US* for higher education since the 1970s, started by President Nixon's rapprochement to China in 1972 and later encouraged by Deng Xiaoping during his term in office.

Xiaoping reforms centered on what worked. He did not accept that a market economy, which he saw producing wealth for other countries, could only be synchronized with a democratic political system. It could be made to work with a command system as existed in China. So, with slogan in hand, *"black cat or white cat, if it can catch mice, it is a good cat,"* he set out to implement his market-driven reforms.

The results are extraordinary. This clear demonstration that the political and economic strata of a society are unrelated and independent of each other and have no conflicts which would prevent their collusion.

Other countries, such as Vietnam, have followed China with remarkable results raising the question as to whether the most efficient political economy is the command-market one.

II (F) – MILTON FRIEDMAN

"Nothing is as permanent as a temporary government program."
Milton Friedman

Milton Friedman (1912–2006), Nobel Prize recipient and the ideological leader of the Chicago School of Economics, is known for his ardent support of free enterprise and the employment of macroeconomic monetary policies, known as *Monetarism*, to regulate the economy. Central Banks in America and Western Economies have largely adopted monetarists theories but have not been cautious, as advocated by Friedman, in say, increasing the money supply. Friedman expressed a preference for small expansions in the money supply to avoid inflationary pressures, but this caution has been totally disregarded by Central Banks, and instead, are providing massive money supply support to the banking industry.

The first monetarist was Richard Cantillon, an 18th century European political economist. Cantillon is known for his position that original recipients of new money enjoy higher standards of living than later recipients. This concept of relative inflation from increases in the money supply and its disproportionate impact on different goods in an economy is referred to as the *Cantillon Effect*. Many analysts use this to explain why asset prices, assets being the original recipients of new money, are affected by an increase in the money supply, instead of households it eventually trickles down to and which increased consumption result in increases to the country's *CPI* prices.

Friedman's Book, *Capitalism and Freedom*, lays out his views that political and economic freedoms are necessary conditions for progress having benefitted from real dissent and exchange of ideas. The role of governments in the political economy should be very limited to enforcement of laws, order, and rights, to be able to regulate companies with market power, and have control over money. The country's Central Bank, the primary controller of money, should be able to increase its supply by 3% to 5% annually to support growth.

Though a monetarist, Freidman was not supportive of Bretton Woods or the gold standard, preferring the current system of floating exchange rates. A standard backed by an asset or precious metal provides a country with more stability in its balance of trade as negative balances would lead to a diminishing of the stock of the precious metal and thus the depreciation of the country's currency. A lower currency would prompt increased demand for the products used, in exchange for restoring their value. Friedman believed the removal of trade barriers, such as quotas and duties, would have a similar effect of stabilizing trade between countries. Friedman opposed the Keynesian fiscal stimulus measures and continual government spending to keep the economy growing. Not surprisingly, the US Ronald Reagan and UK Margaret Thatcher utilized his services in paring down the role of government in their economies. He was able to demonstrate that the rise in government expenditures in an economy was similar to the rise in GDP, demonstrating the absence of a multiplier effect which, if present, would have increased the growth of GDP by a higher ratio.

On taxing of income, Friedman opposed a progressive tax system as unworkable because the rich can take advantage of numerous deductions and reduce their tax liability. His solution is a flat tax for everyone, not burdened by deductions, and through which the rich would pay more, simply because their incomes were higher. It is not the regulation of the rate that increases the obligation on the rich but the level of the income they earn. He was also opposed to welfare programs as being misguided and inefficient, preferring instead a negative income tax for the poor which would provide them with a guaranteed minimum income. Freidman, therefore, became a proponent of a *Universal Basic Income* program, but only for the poor.

III

STAKEHOLDERS

IN THE MAJOR two political economies, democratic-market and command-market, the stakeholders are the same. The third, command-centrally planned, the investor component would be missing. For the most part, households drive the system by creating the demand for goods and services, and the need for rules and structures under which they function as a society. These needs are met by suppliers and investors, and by an oversight governmental structure that facilitates households' access to satisfying them. Unfortunately, those occupying governmental structures, whether freely elected to office or not, are not generally working in the best interest of these households but for the self-aggrandizement of themselves and their cabals. This is expanded on later in the book, but this chapter looks at each contribution to the political economy.

III (A) – HOUSEHOLDS

In the USA, there are 130 million households and since 1990 they have grown annually by approximately 1%. This growth rate is about half of what it was for the prior thirty years. And the size of the household decreased over the last 30 years by 5%. Real income per household has

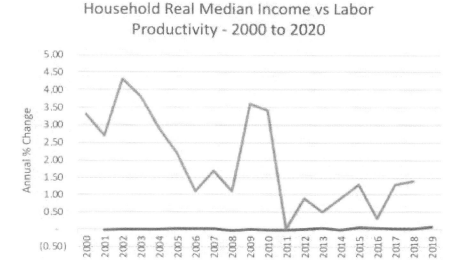

Figure 2 **Developed from US Census Bureau & BLS data.**

been relatively flat, increasing from $63,292 in 2000 to $67,521, 20 years later, an increase under 7% (the increase to 2019, a non-pandemic influenced year, was 10% or an annual increase of one-half of one percent). This anemic growth despite modest growth in labor productivity (see **Figure 2**) is troubling for the American labor force and indicative of the magnitude by which it is over-priced when compared to the global marketplace. Countries to which American manufacturing has been outsourced, China, India, Mexico, Vietnam, all have minimum wage rates significantly lower than the *US*. India, with the lowest hourly rate at $1.47, is one-fifth that of the *US*, which rate of $7.25 per hour, established in 2009, has been exceeded by most industries and States due to it longevity. As the *US* worker productivity cannot compensate for the gap in wage rates, efforts to attract industry back to the *US* is just an unrealistic expectation, with a few exceptions of capital-intensive operations.

Another disturbing aspect of American households is the lack of savings and growing debt. In a 2022 survey, the Board of Governors of the *Federal Reserve System*, found that 37% of respondents couldn't pay an incidental of $400 without resorting to a credit card loan, borrowing from friend or family member, selling something, or just simply couldn't pay it. This ratio was similar to the results of the survey done in 2019, the last pre-pandemic year, but showed an improvement over that of 2013 (50%) when these surveys started. Marginal improvements were seen in 2020 (36%) and 2021 (32%), pandemic years, probably helped by lower spending during lockdowns and the government relief programs. Other surveys seem to confirm this dire state of the American household. It was reported in 2022 that a recent survey by OnePoll conducted on behalf of AmeriLife, found it difficult for Americans to save as 7 out of 10 were living paycheck to paycheck. As savings in any economy are essential for investment to take place, a low savings rate is symptomatic of future contraction. Although the savings rate has been low for some time, the American economy has been able to forestall the consequences by monetizing the economy, a strategy with an expiry date.

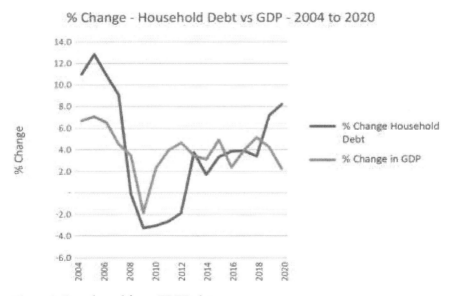

Figure 3 **Developed from FRED data.**

Other troubling characteristics of the American household is the amount of debt it carries. In 2021, household debt stood at $15.85 trillion, having doubled over the last 2 decades. But since debt is the consumption of future income, when the future becomes the present and wages continue to stagnate, servicing these debts will be a major problem requiring larger doses of debt to cope. Already there are signs of distress and calls for debt forgiveness, especially with respect to student loans, are growing. In addition, it is households that drive *GDP* with its demand and spending. When much of that spending is based on debt, the soundness of *GDP* is questionable. From **Figure 3**, one can clearly see a correlation between the change in household debt and that of *GDP*. The divergence in 2020 where *GDP* declined was likely due to the pandemic lockdowns.

The distribution of a nation's wealth is also a key indicator of wellbeing. The *OECD*, a group of mostly rich countries, uses the Gini coefficient to compare income and wealth inequality over time and among nations. This coefficient ranges between 0 and 1, 0 representing perfect equality and 1, completely unequal. Some consider a range of 0.2 to 0.3 to be preferred, but one of 0.3 to 0.4, is considered the outer limit.

The *US* Income Gini coefficient for 2022 was 0.411, on the high side and higher than Western European countries such as France (0.324), Germany (0.317), *UK* (0.351), Finland and Denmark (0.277), and Sweden (0.293). Over the past ten years, the *US* rate has been inching up from 0.40 in 2010 to 0.411 in 2022. The Wealth Gini coefficient is more revealing of the level of inequality in the *US*. The World Economic Forum in 2019, reported that the *US* wealth coefficient was 0.852 with only three countries with higher values (see **Figure 4**). Of interest is that most countries within the top ten for income inequalities are in Africa. This does not translate into wealth gaps in those countries, likely due to a lack of capital markets for the wealthy to park their wealth.

The Gini data confirms other data reviewed about *US* households living paycheck to paycheck and having meagre savings. Its undesirability lies with its curb of demand as the wealthy whose needs/wants have

Highest Net Income Gini Index (%)			Highest Wealth Gini Index (%)		
Country	Income Index (2022)	Wealth Index (2019)	Country	Wealth Index (2019)	Income Index (2022)
South Africa	63.0	80.6	Netherlands	90.2	29.2
Namibia	59.1	78.8	Russia	87.9	37.5
Suriname	57.9	83.2	Sweden	86.7	29.3
Zambia	57.1	79.8	United States	85.2	41.1
Sao Tome	56.3	67.4	Brazil	84.9	48.9
Central African Republic	56.2	77.7	Ukraine	84.7	25.6
Eswatini	54.6	-	Thailand	84.6	35.0
Mozambique	54.0	71.6	Denmark	83.8	27.7
Brazil	48.9	84.9	Philippines	83.7	42.3
Botswana	53.3	80.0	Saudi Arabia	83.4	45.9

Figure 4

Source: **World Economic Forum & World Bank, 2022 report; Credit Suisse, 2019**

already been met, has very little incentive to spend its vast reserve of incomes. Were some of these surpluses redistributed to the less affluent, most of it would go towards increasing the demand for goods and services.

So, *US* households aren't in good shape and cracks are starting to show. Sloganeering such as *"Make America Great Again"*, not solutions, is on the rise, so are suicides, addiction, alcoholism, and declining marriage. In their book, *Deaths of Despair and The Future of Capitalism,* economists Anne Case and Angus Deaton made the case that *US* workers are increasingly losing hope in their future and consequently, mortality rates stopped falling and are rising. Unless a reset takes place soon, these workers comprising American households, will face a lot more hardships and disruptions.

III (B) – COMMERCE & INDUSTRY

This is the sector of the economy that provides the private goods and services needed. The three sub-sectors considered here are — agriculture, manufacture, and services. These sub-sectors operate in highly capitalized financial and commodity markets, which for the *US* are The New York Stock Exchange, Silicon Valley, and the Chicago Mercantile Exchange. Unfortunately, markets in the *US* have become very speculative, not unlike a casino, prompting Keynes to observe *"It is usually agreed that casinos should, in the public interest, be inaccessible and expensive. And perhaps the same is true of Stock Exchanges"* (Calibre e-Books 0.8.63, December 13, 1935, John Maynard Keynes "General Theory of Employment, Interest and Money", p. 112). Keynes would not have been surprised to learn that economists are now justifying these speculations with the use of models. The inverted yield curve occurs when a longer-term security, such as a ten-year note, carries a lower yield than a shorter-term one, such as a 3-month treasury bill. Obviously, this is not what one would expect as longer-term securities carry greater risks and therefore require higher yields to compensate. So, when the yields flip, their relationship is described as *"inverted"*. The only condition explained by an inverted yield curve is a deflationary future caused by a recession. But these are calls made by investors betting on the future and analysts use such outcomes to make recommendations as if factual. Speculation accepted as fact. They even develop econometric models to support their speculation. Such speculations along with short trading, have turned asset markets into forms of gambling places, characterized by large swings in prices over very short periods of time, and diminishing their value to accurately price assets. Wide swings in assets are also a characteristic of asset bubbles where values and prices of assets are not synchronized.

Agriculture

Agricultural societies, those that employ sizable resources in providing food security they need, are generally considered *'less developed'* and the route all societies must take. But as they move through 'developing' and *'developed'* stages of improvement, productivity increases significantly resulting in a combination of reduced inputs and increased output. This was certainly the case with American agriculture.

According to the *US Department of Agriculture*, there are 2.01 million farms in 2021, down from 6.8 million in 1935, but output nearly tripled between 1948 and 2019. This attests to the tremendous productivity in the industry from innovation in animal and crop genetics, labor substitution, chemical development, and farm organization. Corn and soybeans are the major crops grown, in terms of cash receipts, and are used in multiple applications for food, animal feed, biofuels, oils, etc. With respect to animal production, cattle lead the way with 38% of

2020 US Crop & Animal/Animal Product Cash Receipts					
Crop	*Cash Receipt ($ billion)*	*%*	*Animal & Products*	*Cash Receipt ($ billion)*	*%*
Corn	47.8	24	Cattle	63.1	38
Soybeans	41.5	21	Dairy	40.5	25
Fruits & Nuts	28.1	14	Hogs	19.2	12
Vegetables & Melons	18.2	09	Poultry & Eggs	35.5	22
Wheat	08.9	04	All Other	06.6	04
Cotton	07.0	04			
Hay	07.3	04			
All Other	39.8	20			

Figure 5

Source: **USDA Farming & Farm Income**

all animal and animal products production, followed by dairy (25%) and poultry/egg production (22%) (**Figure 5**).

US agriculture is heavily subsidized, but the benefits are not evenly distributed among the farming community, with corn, soybean, and wheat, representing large farm-holders, receiving the bulk of the subsidies. Subsidies were set at $16.5 billion in 2002 but by 2020 had increased to $25 billion. The intent was to help farmers manage the variations in agricultural production due mainly to weather vagaries. These subsidies, which account for 20% of farm income, are the reason the median total income among all farm households ($80,060 in 2020) exceeded the median total household income for the US ($67,521 in 2020).

US farming contributed $134.7 billion to GDP in 2020, or around 0.6%. It is a small, but important part of the economy. Its high level of subsidies distorts the price signals for value-added food and beverage products leading to overconsumption and waste. This is another example of government intervention distorting the proper functioning of the market.

Manufacture

Manufacture is the activity of adding value to raw materials produced by their agriculture and mining sectors. It is characteristic of developing countries providing the absorption of rural labor surpluses from improved productivity in the agriculture sector. The Industrial Revolution, which began in Europe around the mid-eighteen century, started the transformation from rural agricultural societies to urbanized, manufacturing ones.

Improvements in manufacturing depend on major technological breakthroughs. During the mid-18th century industrial revolution, the technology that allowed scale improvements from small craft enterprises was water and steam power. Coal was an important primary energy source in the production of steam. But by the late 1800s, a more efficient form of energy, both in production and distribution, electricity, came to the fore and gave manufacturing a tremendous boost. Electric machines replaced or supplemented labor increasing its productivity. This was further augmented by the internal combustion engine transforming transportation from animal-provided to machine. Other technological advancements since then included the introduction of computers to speed up processes and reduce errors, internet and wireless communications, robotics, and Artificial Intelligence. Labor, therefore, is in competition with all these changes to the manufacturing process and, at least in the US, is losing out because it is overpriced due to labor union and minimum-wage restrictions to the market determined wage rate. Labor is constantly being outsourced to countries with lower wage rates and to Artificial Intelligence.

Currently, the US is the third largest manufacturer worldwide behind China and the European Union. But its labor force has been declining over the last forty years from a peak of 19.4 million in 1979 to 12.8 million in 2019. But despite declines in labor-force participation, US manufacturing output has been increasing from $1.379 trillion in 1997 to $2.342 trillion in 2019, supporting increases in labor productivity through its rapid displacement by capital and technology.

For workers, manufacturing jobs were the driver to middle-class status after World War II, energized by political policies favorable to labor, a major constituent, and lack of global competition. However, the normalization of relations between the US and China by then President, Richard Nixon, in 1972, and China's ascendency to the WTO in 2001, changed the equation. As China modernized its economy under Deng Xiaoping, and not saddled with restrictive labor policies, it quickly became the manufacturing hub of the World. As manufacturing jobs are fungible, they started exiting the US, a high-wage country, for countries with lower wage costs. For the US, the decline was steep during the 2001 to 2009 period, when manufacturing jobs skidded from 17.1 million in January 2001 to 11.5 million in December 2009.

Manufacturing will no longer provide the *US* secondary-educated worker with a comfortable lifestyle as it did until the mid-1980s. Off-shoring and outsourcing to technology have stagnated wages in an economy targeted with inflation every year. It's another illustration of how political interference in the functioning of the market can go terribly wrong with significant consequences to people's lives.

A word on globalization. Globalization is the unfettered movement of goods and capital between countries, without tariff barriers to distort their comparative advantage whether natural, such as minerals, metals, and arable land, or not, such as technology-development. It has positive effects on countries as it did by lifting masses of Chinese workers out of poverty and stabilizing inflationary pressures in the *US* from business cycles.

Unfortunately, globalization is now in decline in Western countries as measures to provide employment opportunities to their citizens invariably means shutting out cheaper foreign-made goods with tariffs and the portrayal of countries progressing as threats to the local workers. Displacement of cheaper goods with those locally made using high-priced labor is inflationary, which will destroy the Western economies. The solution, which has its agonizing costs, is the reduction of these countries' high cost of living by deflationary measures. The chance of this occurring is minimal due to the political cost.

Services

As societies become more developed, that development is concentrated in the provision of services. This seems to be the case with the *US* economy in which in 2019, 78.74% of the workforce was employed in the service sector, 19.91% in industry and 1.36% in agriculture. Another reason for this massive concentration may be that service jobs, except for Information Technology, are not easily offshored. There is some evidence of technology outsourcing as labor pressure for minimum-wage threshold increases.

Data-driven algorithms designed to displace professional workers in the journalistic, legal, and medical fields are on the horizon along with autonomous-driven vehicles used in transportation. In addition, the technological disruptions will continue down to the menial jobs and as we have seen in the case of Whole Foods, where the retail experience will be provided without any worker intervention. This evolution will continue to worsen the worker-condition.

The service economy includes education, health care, information technology, hospitality, financial services, and distribution. As expected, due to its size and scope, the service sector contributed $16.6 trillion to *GDP* and $706 billion to exports in 2019 and employed 190.8 million workers in 2020. But to be competitive on trade deals, and with labor costs rising, the sector will have to undergo a significant transformation to technology idling many workers as offshoring/outsourcing did to manufacturing jobs. Labor displacement on a large scale can be expected in the future for this sector.

III (C) – INVESTORS

There are two types of investors, institutional and retail, the main difference being one of scale. Institutional investing can move markets whereas retail cannot, unless there is retail collaboration as was done in the January 2021 short squeeze on the GameStop stock, causing major financial consequences to hedge funds and short sellers. Morgan Stanley estimates that retail investors make up 10% of the daily trades.

Retail investors work for themselves whereas institutional investors offer their clients brokerage and financial management services for a variety of products with different risk attributes. These products include stocks (ownership shares of public-traded companies), bonds (loans to corporations and government agencies repayable with interest payments), mutual funds (pooling of investor funds for investment in financial instruments that promote a specific strategy), pension funds, hedge funds (investments for the management of risks), and more. The purpose here is not to expand on investors and their various investment products/services, but to capture the importance of this sub-sector and how it is impacted by the *US* political economy.

The Upshot (Jan 26, 2021) reported that *"Using the broadest definition of Wall Street involvement, which includes everything from workplace 401(k)s to personal IRAs, mutual funds and pension holdings, just over half of American families have at least one financial account tied to the market, while just one in six report direct ownership of stock shares."* So, most Americans depend on financial instruments for savings and wealth development although the distribution is highly skewed. In 2019, the top 1 percent of Americans controlled about 38 percent of the value of financial accounts holding stocks. When widened to include the top 10 percent, this climbs to 84%.

Besides the ownership of this wealth, its magnitude is important. The market capitalization of financial assets is estimated to be 230% of *GDP*, somewhat overstated by the asset bubble created by the *US Fed* from its *Quantitative Easing* program.

III (D) – GOVERNMENT

Representative government, the dominant form of political authority today, started as a political instrument to serve the interests of ruling monarchs. And its evolution over several centuries has led to changes in form and authority but not necessarily to its intended benefactors. One change incorporated in governing structures, such as the *US*, estimated to make up to 40% of countries' legislatures, is bicameralism where the legislative body is bifurcated into two chambers, one representing the interest of the people and elected by popular vote, and the other by some less democratic process. In the *US*, the Senate, the lessor democratic bicameral legislative structure, has its undemocratic process further exacerbated by a members' supported feature, which requires a minimum of 60% Senators to accent to certain bills, known as the filibuster. In 2022, the *US Senate* was evenly split among the two major parties with 50 members each, but one party had a majority of 41 million popular votes or 13% more than the other, characterizing its undemocratic nature.

The rationale given for this form of structure is the need for checks and balances the less democratic body imposes over the body of elected representatives, or a clear mistrust of the value of a democratic system. But even the chamber of elected representatives doesn't reflect the concept of *'one man, one vote'* due to *'gerrymandering'*, a process on manipulating the boundaries of districts to increase the chances of a given electoral outcome, by partisan interests, and acceptance of plurality results. In the latter, candidates are declared winners with minority votes, leading to the possibility of minority government. Some countries have addressed this deficiency in their system by requiring runoff elections between the two top vote getters.

As elected officials in these government systems have no obligations to fulfill promises made before their election and can promote their own self-interests once elected, legislators tend to be beholden to lobbyists of special interests and moneyed influences, who in turn provide the funding for their reelection campaigns. Often the lobbyists and influencers' interests are at odds with those of the electorate which are ignored or marginalized. A New York Times investigation done around mid-2022, found that many congressional politicians take advantage of the knowledge and information available to them from exposure to intelligence reports, meetings with CEOs, and their participation in setting the rules of the economy workings, to enrich themselves and families. The resulting stock trades exacerbate many voters' perception that politicians put their own interests above those of the public and Country. A clear failure of a democratic institution to deliver results to its people.

A primary motivation of politicians is reelection, and many spend copious amounts of time raising funds for this process. Others pursue policies damaging the economy but popular with the electorate. One such policy is tax cuts whether justified or not. Since the 1980s, *US* Republican Presidents and their legislative supporters have made it compulsory to reduce the size of the federal government by slashing taxes but not accompanied by a comparable reduction in spending. Accordingly, budget deficits by the Treasury are at all-time high, the size of government hasn't changed, and public debt keeps racking up.

Another reelection ruse is modestly inflating the economy whether as a target or because of increasing public debt. Inflation reduces the cost of debt as each amortization is made with cheaper and depreciated money. It encourages debt such as mortgages and big-item purchases giving the feeling of improved wellbeing. But even the targeted inflation of the *Fed*, set at an arbitrary 2%, doubles the cost-of-living every 35 years, a feature of the *US* economy causing its labor to be overpriced and uncompetitive with offshoring and technology. So, the Country ends up with a long-term problem, but in the short-term, politicians get reelected from a satisfied electorate with the false conviction that it is better off from its ability to acquire more stuff.

Inflation is also a hidden tax with less objectionable openings than a direct tax. Direct tax increases, whether to income, wealth, or consumption, are part of a process of competing interests and can be messy in their justifications. Politicians abhor such processes as they stand to divide opinions and therefore the perception of the contributions they are making. It's generally a lot easier to fund these increased expenditures through debt than direct taxation, and tax the electorate from the resulting inflation. Unfortunately, the electorate doesn't seem to focus on the connection between public debt and inflation and seems unconcerned as labor-market restrictions make them poorer.

The debt-driven inflation referred to above is not debt funded from savings, but debt funded from increases in the money supply, a growing feature of the *US* economy. Money supply debt increasing bank reserves tends to first inflate capital goods due to the Cantillon Effect[8] before trickling down to consumer goods. Except for referring to this phenomenon as an asset bubble, it is generally ignored as if it sorts itself out with consequences only to the wealthy. That's the case when the money supply is managed by the *Fed*. But when the money supply is increased to fund fiscal programs sponsored by the *US Treasury*, as was done to mitigate the impacts of the 2020–2022 pandemic, that becomes a different kettle of fish. These direct disbursements into the pockets of consumers and households increase the demand for consumer goods and services and are captured in the main index of inflation, the Consumer Price Index.

The politicians seem to be personally benefiting from their elected positions. Open Secrets, using data from lawmakers Personal Financial Disclosure filings, concluded that Congress is not only an exclusive club, but a wealthy one. It found that in 2012, for the first time, most members were millionaires, and that trend continued in 2019. And a study done by Ballotpedia using 2004 to 2012 data from the same disclosure forms, found that the inflation-adjusted assets of all members of Congress increased by 15.4% compared to a 3.7% increase for American households. So, members of Congress, who are accountable to lobbyists and other special-interest groups, appear to be doing quite well personally, better than the electorate they are supposedly representing. The discussion so far has been on the *US* legislative branch of government and those who occupy the positions offered there. The executive branch, headed by an elected president, has similar characteristics to the bicameral legislature as the president bears no difference to the legislators and in several cases had origins from this branch.

---

8 An uneven change in relative prices resulting from a change in money supply, which was first described by 18th-century Irish-French economist Richard Cantillon.

The *US* executive branch also suffers from undemocratic outcomes of the legislative branch and the president can be elected on a minority vote count. The executive branch signs legislative proposals into law and its imprimatur and bully pulpit are used to provide the nation with guidance on domestic and foreign initiatives, direction, and decision-making.

The third branch of the *US* federal government is the judicial, where the less democratic chamber of its legislature is charged with selecting the judges of the Country, including that of its Supreme Court. This court, the highest court of the land, has the power of judicial review, the process of determining the consistency of an act with the constitution. The justices on this Court are allowed by the Constitution to "hold their offices during good behavior", interpreted to provide them with lifetime tenure, if they so choose subject only to impeachment. And since 1869, an Act has limited its size to nine members.

As members of the Supreme Court are selected in a political process, the reasoning behind lifetime tenure, that of judicial independence, is ludicrous. Recent rulings by it bear this out as it has moved to support the policies of the political party that nominated its majority on cultural, religious and climate issues.

Although not an official part a government's separation of powers into executive, legislative, and judicial branches, which has been referred to as the three estates, a fourth can be added to institutions that maintain democratic order, the free press or the fourth estate. The fourth estate is operated by the private sector and has the effect of informing, advocating, and framing political issues for the electorate. But that is now changing for the worst driven by private media influence and competitiveness, and the advent of social media. The media, and especially social media, has become the source of much misinformation and conspiracies, protected in 1996 by the adding of new Section 230 to the Communications Act of 1934, coupled with the *Digital Millennium Copyright Act (DMCA)* of 1998. These Acts gave protection to social media companies to operate as intermediaries of content without fear of being liable for that content if they take reasonable steps to delete or prevent access. The fourth estate is not only creating divisions in opinions but is hardening them through confirmation bias.

In summary, the *US* government is failing its people by representing the special interests of moneyed-groups and self-interests of its politicians. This was confirmed by an extensive study using 20 years of data, done by Professors Martin Gilens (Princeton University) and Benjamin I. Page (Northwestern University)[9]. They concluded that the *US* government does not represent the interest of its people and that the opinions of 90% of Americans have essentially no impact on policymaking. Short-term measures with long-term dire ramifications, such as unsustainable debt, and debasing its currency through uncontrolled increases in the money supply, will not end well. Debts which cannot be repaid would have to be absorbed by their creditors, and worthless money would need to be backed by value.

Winston Churchill cynically stated that "democracy is the worst form of government, except for all the others that have been tried." Perhaps he had in mind that such a system is sub-optimal as it gives equal weight to the opinions of the uneducated as to the erudite in society — the rationale for the checks and balances of the bicameral legislatures in so many countries.

Perhaps presidential candidate Hillary Clinton had this defect in mind when in September 2016 and during the heat of a campaign, she referred to her opponent's supporters, as a *'basket of deplorables'* because of their lack of education and their identification with hate groups. But when not only the unknowledgeable opinions are being ignored by the political process but most of its electorate, the system of governance is not working and will have serious implications for the future of all.

---

9 Gilens, M., & Page, B. (2014). Testing Theories of American Politics: Elites, Interest Groups, and Average Citizens. *Perspectives on Politics, 12*(3), 564–581. doi:10.1017/S1537592714001595.

III (E) – CENTRAL BANKS

In the *USA*, the role of its central bank is performed by the *Federal Reserve System (FRS or Fed)*, comprising twelve reserve banks, and created on December 23, 1913, by the *Federal Reserve Act*. Its creation came during a time of financial panics justifying the need for central control of the monetary system. Its mandate is to maximize employment, stabilize prices and moderate long-term interest rates, but it has broadened its responsibilities since then.

The *FRS* is unique among central banks as it is owned by the nationally chartered commercial banks, which elect board members and receive dividends. It is entirely funded by earned revenues from which it covers costs and pays dividends, but all surplus revenues are transferred to the *US Treasury*. Its decision making is independent and cannot be changed by the executive or legislative branches of government.

Needing to provide confidence and prevent bank runs (rapid withdrawal of deposits from a bank due to perceived uncertainty), the FRS functions as a transaction-clearing house, and lender of last resort. Through these two facilities, stability is maintained as the *Fed* adjusts the liquidity of member banks, at a cost, from its vast resources. An important function is the maintenance of the reserve requirements of private banks. These are the ratio of deposits the *Fed* requires these banks to retain in their lending portfolios to reduce the risk that banks would be unable to meet withdrawals from depositors during normal operations. So, if the reserve requirement for banks, set by the *Fed*, is 10%, banks are limited to lending a maximum of 90% of their deposits. Banks which carry reserves more than the requirement can lend these surpluses to other banks on a short-term basis and for the purpose of maintaining the requirements. Monetary policy is partly shaped by the *Fed* influencing the interest rate of these short-term funds as it will also pay the banks interest on these surpluses.

The most important policy setting group at the FRS is its *Federal Open Market Committee (FOMC)* comprising members from both the board of governors and regional banks. It sets policy on open market operations (*OMO*), the major monetary tool available to the *Fed*. *OMO* is the practice of buying and selling *US Treasury* and other securities to regulate the money supply placed in the reserves of *US* banks. A key rate set by the board of governors, as a target, is the *federal funds rate*, the rate banks charge each other for short-term loans. The *Fed* believes that the level of this rate will keep the economy on an even keel. FOMC is then charged with keeping the *federal funds rate* at this targeted level and it does this through its *OMO*. So, if the targeted *federal funds rate* is below the actual rate, the *Fed* would purchase these securities from primary dealers on the open market (competitive bidding) and by so doing, increase the reserves of member banks/primary dealers. Their larger reserves lead to the lowering of the actual rate, and this will continue until the target is achieved. This lower rate also influences other interest rates with longer terms. Selling securities would have the opposite effect.

Keynes seemed supportive of the *Fed* setting these rates with different maturities rather than influencing their levels. In his *General Theory of Employment, Interest & Money*, he opines, *"Perhaps a complex offer by the Central Bank to buy and sell at stated prices gilt-edged bonds of all maturities in place of a single bank rate for short-term bills, is the most important practical improvement which can be made in the technique of monetary management."*[10]

The *Fed* also uses its discount window to lend directly to member banks but discourages this option by charging a hefty markup on interest over the *federal funds rate*.

But since the Global Financial Crisis of 2007–2008, the *Fed* has greatly increased the monetary tools for stabilizing the economy by adding liquidity. Generally, these new tools are modifications of its *FOMC* and

---

10 Keynes, John Maynard, 1883–1946. The General Theory of Employment, Interest and Money. London: Macmillan, 1936.

Discount Window activities by extending the length of transactions, types of collaterals and eligible borrowers.

The *Fed* also targets the inflation rate, in this case the core personal consumption expenditure index, currently at about 2%. As increasing the money supply without increasing output is the definition of inflation, this allows the *Fed* to gauge how much *Quantitative Easing* is tolerable in the economy. If in its expansion program, it finds that the inflation target is being exceeded, it is a sign that it needs to pull back on the money supply.

So, the *Fed*'s role in the economy is that of a central planner, influencing the level of the money supply, interest, and inflation rates and by so doing, usurping the role of the market. No longer are interest rates set by the level of savings but by arbitrary targets established by the *Fed*. The money supply is then manipulated to try to meet both interest and inflation targets.

But under the current banking structure, Central Banks are not the only entities, seemingly (see technical note below for clarification), increasing the currency supply in the economy. Commercial banks do so under a fractional reserve lending system. So, if the reserve requirement is set at 10% of deposits, a commercial bank is allowed to lend 90% of its deposits. This lending produces additional deposits in the banking system permitting further lending of 90% of their value or on the second iteration, in this example, 81% of the original value of the amount deposited. By this and its continuation, the Nation's currency supply appears to increase without participation of the Central Bank. The Central Bank can influence the magnitude of this supply by varying the reserve requirement rate, and in the *US*, has been known to set this rate, at the start of the *COVID* pandemic, at zero.

A technical note: Commercial banks cannot increase a Country's currency supply for only the Central Bank can do so. In effect commercial banks, through their lending practices, are increasing the velocity of the supply, which has similar impacts to the economy as increases in the supply.

Further, the *Fed* is known to dabble in unchartered waters during emergencies and especially during disruptions such as that caused by *COVID*. Its balance sheet increased from $870 billion in August 2007 to a whopping $8.97 trillion in June 2022. The *Fed* balance sheet then comprised bank deposits and treasury securities ($4.6 trillion), federal reserve notes or money in circulation ($2.22 trillion) and reverse repurchase agreements ($2.04 trillion). Normalization of such a magnitude has not taken place before and consequences are unknown. Distortion from this much stimulus, referred to as *Quantitative Easing* but officially termed *Large Scale Asset Purchase Programs (LSAPs)*, are evident. The 30-year fixed mortgage rate dipped as low as 2.65% in January 2021, way below the historic rate of 8.1% (1990s) the last normal decade free of central bank interventions, and 6.2% (2000s) in the decade of the great recession and the central bank interference that came with it. Lending money at 2.65% with an inflation target of 2% disincentives savings and cheapens the time-value of money.

As the evidence from the monetarists is that such monetary measures do affect the performance of the economy, then the *Fed* are central planners akin to those of Eastern Europe's Soviet States. And because it does not monitor asset inflation, a major characteristic of *Quantitative Easing*, it fails to recognize the damage its policies are having on the economy.

IV

ECONOMIC PARAMETERS

THESE ARE THE measures in a political economy that drive policy decisions by the political directorate. When properly managed and basically left to the notions of the market with government offering limited inducements and regulation to ensure safety and to protect market conditions from rent-seeking interests, these economic parameters will result in improved wellbeing and peace for any country and its peoples. But when violated by politicians and corporations for their self-serving interests, when corporations become too big to fail, and overindulgence leads to half measures at correction, such as "*soft landings,*" the roots of economic destruction are being sown and will likely lead to desperation and conflict among its peoples.

IV (A) – MONEY & CURRENCY

"Paper money eventually returns to its intrinsic value: zero."

Voltaire

Although "money" and "currency" are used interchangeably by many analysts, they are not the same. money is a more general term of a medium of exchange between anything that's exchangeable. With money, no longer does one have to barter/exchange a goat for a table, or any of the numerous imprecise dealings that would accrue without it, to satisfy wants and needs with those possessions. Money, representing one's parted accumulated possessions and labor, can be more precise in representing value obtained for value given up.

Money is understood to have three attributes for it to meet its function. It should be a *"unit of account"* meaning that the value of items can be measured in a standard common denominator, a measure of the monetary unit, for without it, such measurement would be most difficult. Second, is a *"medium of exchange"*, a measure as an intermediary instrument that facilitates the exchange of goods among parties with a precise understanding of the value of these goods. And third, a *"store of value"* representing the accumulated possessions and labor given up in delay of consumption. Keynes introduced a fourth attribute when he described money as having a *"standard of value"*. *"The fact that money has low elasticities of production and substitution, and low carrying-costs tends to raise the expectation that money-wages will be relatively stable; and this expectation enhances money's liquidity-premium and prevents the exceptional correlation between the money-rate of interest and the marginal efficiency of other assets which might, if it could exist, rob the money-rate of interest of its sting."* (General Theory, P. 165). In other words, the peculiarities of money make it a substitute for other assets in liquidity and the money-rate of interest.

The classical economists ignored money altogether treating economics as the study of the optimal allocation of resources, a means to an end. Money played no part in this allocation. But Keynes made money a centerpiece of the discipline and spent much time on money-rate of interest, having considered money an asset.

Currency, which can be in tangible (coins, paper) or intangible (digital) form, is one form of money. Other forms of money used in the past are gold and precious metals. When gold and precious metals are used as money, the money is said to have intrinsic value. When in paper/digital format with no asset backing, its value relies on the faith and thrust in the government authority that issues it. Paper/digital currencies are therefore at risk to the monetary policies of the government entities issuing them and have been known to become worthless in Germany (1922–1923), Hungary (1945–1946), Yugoslavia (1992–1994), Zimbabwe (2007–2008), Venezuela (2016–2018), and many countries in between with similar conditions now (2022), threatening Turkey, Lebanon, and Sri Lanka.

Currency, which is fungible, allows persons/consumers to engage in exchange transactions within a country in addition to trade among countries. An entity in country *"A"* wishing to purchase goods from country *"B"* must first obtain the currency of country *"B"* to do so. This involves foreign exchange rates between the two countries' currencies and can vary on a frequent basis. If the currency of *"B"* is weak and is relatively inexpensive to obtain by *"A"*, the latter's cost-of-living decreases, ceteris paribus, but increases when *"B"* is stronger. So, the currency exchange rates among countries can affect the price levels and cost-of-living conditions just based on the strengths and weaknesses of their currencies.

From 1944 and until 1971, a country's currency was backed by gold having been reaffirmed by the agreement of *Bretton Woods*. The exchange price of gold was then $35 per ounce. Then the *US* started funding its war in Vietnam without the requisite backing and could no longer convert its dollars held by other nations for gold as required by the *Bretton Woods agreement*. The dollar was decoupled from gold thus creating fiat currency, and a main source of its economic problems. So, a financial order based on intrinsic value, crafted by 730 delegates from 44 nations in 1944, was instantaneously eliminated by a *US* President unilateral stroke of a pen in 1971, a single action that is possibly the main cause of the today's world economic problems.

Fortunately for the *US*, it quickly moved thereafter to establish its currency as the world reserve currency and as the *Petrodollar*, requiring all oil and gas sales be priced in *US* dollars. This has allowed it to create dollars from thin air without any consequences to its value due to the international demand for them. Were it not for the status of the dollar, its expanded supply would have certainly resulted in its destruction as a currency.

But besides providing more monetary flexibility, there is no evidence that the use of fiat currency provides a country with benefits such as increases in *GDP*. As it is easier to create and produce, allowing for fiscal profligacy, fiat currency will most likely generate inflationary pressures by its unjustified issuance, as seen in several countries that experienced hyper-inflation from this, but hardly changes in wealth. It is also the source for astronomical and thus unsustainable debt being racked up by many countries. **Figure 6** shows that the ten-year average growth in the *US* per capita *GDP* since the introduction of fiat currency in 1971 has not exceeded the ten-year average prior to its introduction. Soon, the *US* started weaponizing its currency, the *US* Dollar, and which has also

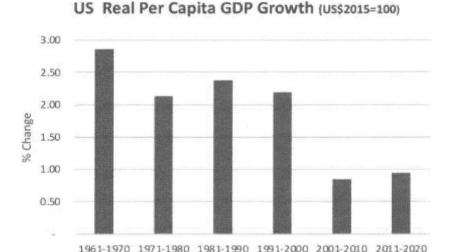

Figure 6

Source: **World Bank**

been accepted since the *Bretton Woods Agreement* as the world reserve currency, to sanction countries which actions it disagreed with. This is possible because settlements to trade agreements are generally in *US* dollars due to the *US$* reserve currency status and Petrodollar agreements. So, to settle an international trade arrangement, one bank, registered by the *Society for Worldwide Interbank Financial Telecommunication (SWIFT)*, has to purchase *US* dollars from a *US* Bank also registered by *SWIFT*. Restricting the transaction as part of the *US* sanctioning process is simply denying the initial bank access to the *SWIFT* messaging system. But as more countries, such as Russia, Iran, and Venezuela, fall under these American-imposed trade sanctions, they are resorting to alternatives that bypass the use of *US* dollars thereby threatening that currency as a future world reserve currency. For example, India is buying petroleum from Russia during the Ukrainian sanctions, paying for these supplies, not in *US* dollars but in rubbles, the currency of Russia. And as the future of money is heading to central bank issued digital currencies (*CBDCs*), it is likely that the *US* dollar, or any single currency, will stop being acceptable to countries as a medium of exchange.

And finally, money as a payment system can be slow and costly. Money transfers enable the payment system of a country, which can be sub-divided into retail, (between and among households and businesses), wholesale, (interbank), and cross-border. Retail transfers are generally accomplished using cash, checks, credit and debit cards, and electronic transfers. Physical payment tools such as cash and checks are fast becoming obsolete, hurried along by the remote shopping and virus avoidance of the *COVID* pandemic, and the electronic tools are on the upswing. In Sweden, cash payments account for less than 10% of all payments, and banks discourage their transactions by charging a premium for cash deposits, which takes up valuable space in their vaults.

Wholesale transactions, usually involving the countries' central banks clearing money instruments comprising checks and electronic transfers, can be slow when using a net settlement system. Such systems net out the movement of funds among banks and adjust their reserves daily. Electronic transfers allow these adjustments in real time, making for a faster and more efficient settlement system. The *US* uses both settlement systems. *Fedwire*, operated by the *Federal Reserve*, is a real time settlement system with more than 5,500 participants and in 2020, handled over 180 million transactions which exceeded $800 trillion.

Cross-border payments are the most time-consuming as currencies with different exchange rates are involved and include banking institutions in the countries engaging in the trade. So, when a roaster in Guyana wants to purchase coffee green beans from Brazil, it must first obtain from its Guyanese bank Brazilian reals and pay the supplier in Brazil by depositing in the supplier's bank account. But what if the purchaser's Guyanese bank does not have reals to sell? The purchaser would then have to obtain a currency acceptable to both countries for payment purposes, such as the *US* dollar, before the transaction can be effected.

Cross-border payments are not only complicated by the number of currencies involved but can be costly by the number of banks the transfers must navigate, and the communications systems needed to ensure the funds get to the intended destination. The various platforms to accomplish this under the current system are slow, costly, difficult to track, and presents great risks to countries' currency values from speculators, thus affecting the relationship between imports and exports.

IV (B) – PRICE INFLATION

"Any increase in the money supply not supported by an increase in the production of goods & services leads to an increase in prices."
                                        Austrian School of Economics

Inflation is the decrease in the purchasing power of a currency from an increase in the general price level of consumer goods and services, and those of assets, both real estate and financial. As the level of commodity and asset prices rise, each monetary unit buys fewer of them.

Inflation is caused by increases in aggregate demand from fiscal and monetary measures, or from supply restrictions brought about by disruptions in weather, from conflicts, and from breakdowns in the supply-chain. So, increases in government deficit spendings funded by increases in the money supply are inflationary (demand pull), as well as the results from major disruptions, such as droughts, in countries which are major energy or raw material suppliers (supply push).

Inflation was a major feature of the American economy occurring in what is termed business cycles, periodic fluctuations between the expansion and contraction of economic output activity. Although it is known that contractions start with decreases in demand leading to decreases in production, employment and income, economists were at odds explaining what triggers the decreases in demand. An obvious culprit is inflation. As expansion occurs, labor rates rise with consequential inflationary pressures, and prior to opening the *US* economy to China and the global marketplace, those pressures were not readily abated leading to downturns.

It is interesting that after 2001, the year China was accepted as a member of the *World Trade Organization (WTO)*, downturns in the *US* economy were not from the general economy but from asset bubbles, sub-prime real estate, and restrictions from a pandemic. Indeed, the downturn in 2001 was also from an asset bubble, the dotcom bubble. That was not the case before 2001. The three prior recessions of 1980, 1981 and 1990 were as a result of *Federal Reserve* policies to bring general inflation down from double-digit levels (1980 & 1981) and to address oil price increases from the invasion of Kuwait by Iraq (1990). Therefore, general price inflation has decreased since 1990 relative to previous periods largely due to trade policies with lower cost nations.

Besides business cycles, general inflation also has other mal effects on an economy, such as increases in the cost of living. The *Federal Reserve* has accepted an arbitrary 2% inflation rate, which has unscientific origins in New Zealand[11], as a target to guide its management of the US money supply. Expansion and contraction of the money supply depends on this target. But any level of general price inflation harms an economy and, even at 2% per annum, the cost-of-living doubles every 35 years. Increases in the cost-of-living makes labor costs uncompetitive to low cost-of-living countries such as Mexico and many Asian countries, encouraging offshoring of jobs, and technology substitutions of labor for those of whom moving would not be practical, such as the work-force in the service sector. Evidence of the latter can be seen at some retail stores such as Whole Foods where there is no labor contribution in completing a transaction, and at airports where passengers now check-in their luggage themselves.

The solution politicians often propose is to pressure companies to locate their operations in the US, and some are responding positively but with the condition of government subsidies. For if a business operation is uncompetitive, it will only go forward if the potential loss from its operation is removed with a subsidy. So, instead of deflating the economy to lower the cost-of-living, and which benefits all workers, the US government chose to increase its deficit spending so that a few may be employed.

IV (C) – PRODUCTIVITY & INNOVATION

"When the winds of change blow, some people build walls and others build windmills."

Ancient Chinese Proverb

11   An off-cuff remark made by the NZ's Finance Minister on a TV show.

Innovation, the development of a new product or service, a different approach and way of thinking, or a new method or process, is essential for increasing productivity, the measure of output from a unit on input. So, productivity is driven by innovation.

Most innovations in a world several millennia old only came within the last several centuries starting with the Industrial Revolution in the 18th Century. The innovation responsible for this new and radical approach, to producing goods and subsequently their transportation, is the steam-powered engine which after perfection, replaced water and wind energy technologies. And a century later, coal-fired steam generators produced commercial electricity, a superior form of energy, to propel productivity.

Besides steam and electrical power, other business-friendly inventions of this period include the internet/computer/smart phone combination which permitted quick communications and payment platforms, marketing strategies using social media, storage, and access/streaming to/of large quantities of data, knowledge, and information. American Companies have led the way with the emerging technologies since the 1960s with Microsoft, Amazon, Apple, Google/Alphabet, and Facebook/Meta filling those slots.

The US is still one of the leading innovative countries worldwide as the next level of technologies move into the realm of neural learning and Artificial Intelligence. The US is well positioned to compete in technologies such as autonomous vehicles, 3-D printing, and factory/warehouse robotics. But this is a double-edged sword, a case for ambivalence. For although innovation and invention are essential for productivity gains, fewer workers are needed to produce the same level of output. Politicians address this retrenchment by promoting unsustainable debt as long as it doesn't blowup while they are in office. But time is of the essence. Consider just one of the many technologies being developed at exponential rates, the autonomous vehicle. As a vehicle serves a single purpose, transportation, there is no need to own one but to summon it when needed, which apps already do. There would be no need for private vehicle parking, freeing up large tracks in urban areas for other development. Autonomous trucks alone will eventually retrench most of the 3.5 million truck drivers the *US Census* estimates ply the Country's highways, which estimate corresponds to the American Trucking Associations 2019 estimate of 3.6 million. Another half million taxi drivers' jobs are at risk. This technology will undoubtedly be disruptive. Already, Americans are starting to despair. In their book *Deaths of Despair: And the Future of Capitalism*, Anne Case and Angus Deaton, two Princeton University Economics Professors, make the case that America's working class is committing suicide at an extraordinary rate, is drug-overdosing and abusing alcohol, from a sense of hopelessness in the future. The American dream is in decline for the white working class as the country has become a land of fewer opportunities for them. Not having a college education and seeing the decline of labor unions, this demographic is seeking alternative solutions as was evident in the country's 2016 Presidential election, followed by events since then, including attempted insurrection at the country's Capitol on January 6, 2021.

As conditions will only worsen due to the new technologies on the horizon, what Malthus refers to as vice will only get worse and overtake the USA.

IV (D) – DEBT

The author's position is that debt is the *advance consumption of future income*, and when not used for investment purposes, will inevitably constrain consumption.

Sometimes, perspectives are useful in understanding the core of a concept such as the author's perception of debt being the consumption of future income for it must be repaid from that source. So, it should only be engaged in when it enhances future income and as an investment in the future. Using debt to fund education or training, to purchase an asset such as a house or car when opportunity costs of housing and transportation are higher than the carrying costs of the debt, to build a highway that opens land to housing when there is homelessness indicating a shortage of affordable units, are all wise ways to deploy debt. Using debt to fund discretionary purchases, for operating costs of a company, or for government support programs, are wasteful ways of employing debt with serious ramifications in the future.

But politicians worldwide aren't concerned with long-term implications but what can continue their hold on public power. They encourage debt through the manipulation of the interest rate (cheapen the cost of debt) and the inflation rate (amortize debt with depreciated money) as this increases nominal *GDP* and a sense of well-being of the electorate. The public debt in the *US* has grown to $31 trillion by 3rd quarter 2022 with household and non-financial corporate debt running at around $15.85 trillion and $12.2 trillion, respectively. The total *US* debt is $58 trillion, and with a *GDP* of $22.4 trillion, the *US* total debt to *GDP* ratio is 2.59 and its public debt is 1.36. It means that the *US* has consumed over two and a half years of future income of which its government, on behalf of its citizens, has consumed 1.36 years. As the income that has been consumed is not required to be repaid in the same amortizations/ quantities as it was when consumed and is actually lower because of agreed delays in its repayment due to benefits accruing creditors from these delays (servicing the debt), the dire ramification of this massive burden is extended into the future.

The *US* is not alone with this destructive practice. Venezuela and Japan have the highest debt to *GDP* ratio in the World with many countries heading down the same rabbit hole. Many of those with the highest public debt to *GDP* ratios, shown in the table at **Figure 7**, are experiencing great economic difficulties directly linked to these liabilities. Those with the lowest ratios are not necessarily better off as some may not have used debt wisely to develop their economies. For some, infrastructure development which could have improved the lives of their populations, went unbuilt because available funds under a debt

Country	Highest Debt/GDP %	Country	Lowest Debt/GDP %
Venezuela	350	Brunei	3.2
Japan	266	Afghanistan	7.8
Sudan	259	Kuwait	11.5
Greece	206	Congo (Dem Rep)	15.2
Lebanon	172	Eswatini	15.5
Cape Verde	157	Burundi	15.9
Italy	156	Palestine	16.4
Libya	155	Russia	17.8
Portugal	134	Botswana	18.2
Singapore	131	Estonia	18.2

Figure 7

Source: World Population Review (2020 data)

program were not available or utilized. Schools and medical facilities were not constructed leading to substandard public education and health care.

The question then is what is the optimal level of public debt when measured to a country's GDP? When US household debt is compared to GDP, or even the income it generates, estimated at between 60% to 70% but on further analyses, most of it is sensible debt (**Figure 8**).

Although total US household debt is approximately 70% of GDP, and the outer range of its contribution, the bulk of it, 73% of it is invested in homes, and an additional 20% in education and transportation, a total of 93% in real estate and services that produce income or exceed opportunity costs. If these returns exceed the cost of debt, including its amortization, then debt was a sensible option.[12]

---

12 It is now known that many students are unable to repay their loans requiring forgiveness, a clear sign that the rewards from their increased knowledge do not adequately compensate for the associated educational costs, and also an indication that US education is overpriced.

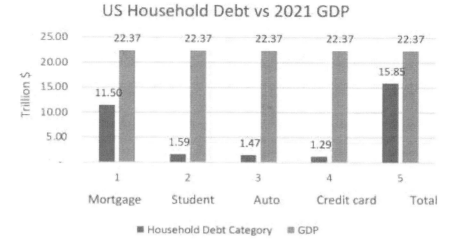

Figure 8

Source: **Federal Reserve Bank of NY**

The *US Federal Budget* has three components — mandatory expenditures, discretionary expenditures, and interest on debt. Generally, mandatory and discretionary expenditures make up 90% of the budget, the total of which before the pandemic was about $4 trillion. During the pandemic years, and because of the support programs from restrictions to the economy, the total *federal budget* grew to $7 trillion, with all increases funded with debt. The *federal budget* does not contain a separate capital budget and includes capital projects in both mandatory and discretionary spending. Therefore, unlike households, analyzing debt by capital and operational outlays is not practical.

If the question of what constitutes an optimal level of debt for any country from a classical economic viewpoint, cost and returns would have to be examined. Classical economists hold that a market is in equilibrium when marginal cost equals marginal price, that is the cost to produce an additional unit of any good or service equals the price someone is willing to pay for it. If the cost was higher, the producer loses income and if lower, stands to gain from the production of additional units.

Applying this to debt, which cost is its amortization, and benefit, the income from its deployment, a rule can be established that debt is optimized when the marginal amortization rate equals the marginal income from the investment made. But this would be messy as the repayment of debt has various methods not associated with amortization — periodic repayment of principal and interest with the latter declining with each subsequent payment — and the timing of cost and income are not synchronized.

A preferred approach is to compare the amount borrowed to the present worth or *net present value (NPV)* of the income stream from the investment supported by the borrower. As an illustration, a government borrows $20 million to build a toll road providing $1.5 million in revenues annually. The loan term is 20 years at a 5% rate of interest, and at the end of the 20-year term, the road has a retention value of $5 million. In this example, the *present worth* of the revenue stream is $20.6 million, almost identical to the loan. It is rational to incur this debt as the users of the road value it as much as its cost to build. If on the other hand, users were only willing to contribute $1 million annually, with its present value being only $14.3 million, a deficit of $5.7 million and thus not a feasible investment.

The bottom line is that debt is generally not justified to cover operating costs as this implies living beyond one's means and will not end well when engaged in by those who are not covering current expenditures from current income sources but are consuming future income for these expenditures. The future, therefore, means increasing debt as income is now diminished by past debt, an unsustainable position.

Some US households have already found themselves in this situation. Peter Coy, a New York Times Correspondent, reported surveys indicating that there are US households earning $250,000 annually which are living paycheck to paycheck, a clear case of the debasement of current income from past debt. And surely the US public debt includes much operating expenditures that should have been covered by public taxes and fees.

Debt is properly incurred without increasing the liability and burden of future generations when limited to investments with measurable social and economic benefits and which can justify the level of debt. The *US* public debt, as well as that of many other countries, does not meet this definition, and has exceeded the capacity of the Nation to repay.

IV (E) – FISCAL & MONETARY POLICIES

"A system of capitalism presumes sound money, not fiat money manipulated by a central bank."

Ron Paul, US Author & Congressman

Fiscal and monetary policies are competing approaches employed by governments to manage macroeconomic conditions of an economy such as *GDP* growth, inflation, and employment. The major proponent of fiscal policies is John Maynard Keynes who held that governments should not depend on the market to correct for business cycles but actively intervene either with deficit spending during downturns or contractionary tax increases during rapid expansion to reduce or prevent inflation. Keynes fiscal theories, which involved massive expenditures on public projects and social welfare programs not supported by tax revenues, were developed in response to the Great Depression, and found to be effective. But countries don't have the discipline to reverse course during times of rapid expansion and to adopt contractionary measures such as tax increases to mitigate potential inflation and cool the economy. Accordingly, Keynes theories were never properly tested and were deemphasized after the stagflation of the 1970s. The gap was filled by monetary policies and their advocate, Milton Friedman. These policies hold that macroeconomic conditions can be adequately managed by manipulating the short-term interest rates and money supply. Monetary policy is generally outside the control of politicians and within the control of the Central Bank, but the lines could be blurred unless there is strict independence of the Central Bank from the political regime. In the United States, the Central Bank, known as the *Federal Reserve Bank*, implements monetary policy through a dual mandate to maximize employment and minimize inflation.

These two approaches, however, will have different effects on the economy. The rapid expansion of the money supply, which went into overdrive during the great recession of 2007/2008, hardly affected the general rise in prices, as measured by the *CPI*, but had a significant impact on asset prices which increases are referred to as a bubble. **Figure 9** compares the percent increase in M2 money supply, the *S&P* average used as a surrogate for asset prices, and the *Consumer Price index (CPI)*. During this time, asset prices demonstrated the inflationary effects of increases in the money supply whereas consumer prices did not. However, in 2021, there is a blip in the *CPI*, not necessarily from the 25% increase in the money supply that year, although that sizable increase would affect the real estate/rental component in the index, but because of fiscal measures that

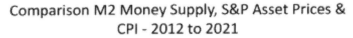

Figure 9

Source: Developed from FRED, S&P and World Bank data

provided support to restrictions from the pandemic. Such measures and programs included workers' unemployment compensation, emergency rent assistance, payments to small businesses to help them maintain their payrolls, and support to local governments. Since 2020, these have increased the federal government expenditures from around $4 trillion to about $7 trillion during the pandemic years. The increase in the *CPI* in 2021 is more related to these fiscal measures, which directly impacts the purchasing power of households, than increases in the money supply. So, inflationary increases in the money supply are largely limited to asset prices, due to the *Cantillon Effect*, a theory according to which those benefitting from the distribution of a currency are those closest to its distribution, such as capital markets, whereas impacts on the *CPI* will result from fiscal measures. This has serious implications for monetary policy as the wrong index, consumer goods prices and not asset prices, is being monitored by the Central Banks to regulate their *GDP decisions* on the magnitude of money supply that can be tolerated in an economy without adverse consequences.

But a broader issue is Central Bank interventions in monetary policy bypassing the efficiency of the marketplace. Interest rates should not be artificially manipulated to bring about a targeted and arbitrarily determined level of inflation, as the consequential level of the money supply will ultimately lead to the debasement of the currency. The *US*, because of the special status of its currency, may take longer than other countries at currency depreciation, but depreciation is inevitable from the oversupply of its money supply. Over the past decade, the *US* money supply has seen increases half the time by double digits, not the modest increases recommended by the monetarist Milton Freidman. The actions of the *US Federal Reserve* amount to central planning of the economy, with all the failures associated with such an approach when the efficiency of the marketplace is abandoned.

IV (F) – THE INTEREST RATE & QUANTITATIVE EASING/TIGHTENING

"Capitalism cherishes voluntary contracts and interest rates that are determined by savings, not credit creation by a central bank."

Ron Paul, US Author & Congressman

Classical economists held that the natural rate of interest is that which preserved equality between the rate of savings and the rate of investment. Keynes' theory is that all capital-assets, including money, had their own rate of interest based on their marginal rate of efficiency. So, one could have a wheat-rate of interest or a copper-rate of interest depending on the asset and its different marginal efficiencies. The asset-rate value is the discount rate which makes the present value of a series of annuities equal to the present supply price of the asset, thus its marginal efficiency. But capital-assets possess three attributes in different degrees – wastage, carrying costs and liquidity premiums/disposal costs – making for their impractical use as a standard of measurement. Keynes concluded that it is the money-rate of interest which is the significant rate of interest because of the peculiarities of a small elasticity of production by private enterprise, as distinct from the monetary authority, a zero elasticity of substitution meaning that as the value of money rises, there is no motive or tendency to substitute some other factor for it, and beyond a certain point money's yields from liquidity is not elastic in its response to an increase in its quantity approaching the yields of other types of assets. Keynes's position doesn't invalidate that of the Classical Economists, it simply takes it through a more arduous routine.

The money-rate of interest is now generally accepted as the cost for a monetary unit of present income over that of future income, or the cost of utility rather than abstinence. Because there is a preference for utility now than later, in a free market, there will always be a positive interest rate. But its levels are not market determined but are influenced by Central Banks as part of their monetary policies. As Central Banks deal in short-term lending, especially among member banks, there are other considerations that make up the longer-term maturity for loans such as the amount of collateral pledged and the perceived riskiness of the borrower. The interest rate banks charge their credit card customers are multiple times that of the *Federal Funds Rate* due to lack of collateral and high default rates of users. As shown in **Figure 10**, increases in the *Federal Funds Rate* do seem to increase that of credit card rates, the difference between the two is the risk premium credit card customers are required to pay to compensate lenders for their losses from defaults. The *federal funds rate*, the interest rate which *US* depository institutions lend reserve balances to other depository institutions overnight, is kept to a tight targeted range set by the *Federal Open Market Committee* and controlled by its *Open Market Operations (OMO)* by adjusting the supply of reserve balances. Since the global financial crisis of 2008, often referred to as the Great Recession or the Global Financial Crisis, these targeted ranges have approached zero as happened between December 2008 and December 2015, and again in March 2020 to March 2022.

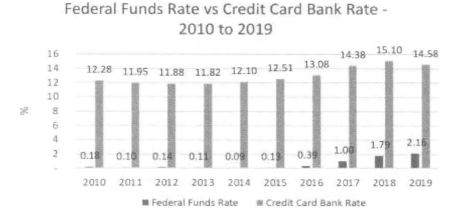

Figure 10

Source: Federal Reserve Bank of St. Louis & Macrotrends

At such low levels, there is not much maneuvering of this rate for further economic stimulus, so the *OMO* turns to another tool, euphemistically termed *Quantitative Easing. Quantitative Easing (QE)* focuses on purchases of government bonds and other securities through its *OMO* to increase the supply of money and liquidity at the banks which would allow them to lower their interest rates, encouraging bank lending and investment. The reverse of *QE* is *Quantitative Tightening*, where Central Banks are forced to change course due to the mal effects of prolonged *QE* on the economy, such as stagflation where inflation and unemployment remain at unacceptable levels.

Other countries have pushed the envelope on *QE*. In Japan, its Central Bank, in the late 1990s, moved from buying government bonds to buying corporate debt and stocks. The Swiss National Bank purchased so many assets that their value exceeded that of the Country's *GDP*, and several years later, the Bank of England joined the band with both government and corporate debt purchases. The *Federal Reserve Bank* followed suit during its *QE* to address the restrictions on the economy from the pandemic.

But the chart also shows a development in monetary central planning not supported by the market, negative real interest rates. For most of the period, the nominal *Federal Funds Rates* were below the rate of inflation, resulting in a negative real rate of interest. This only makes sense during periods of deflation where one's purchasing power is boosted by decreases in the general level of prices. But although the practice of keeping interest rates low at such levels is because the economy is weak and needs to be stimulated, the *Fed* is not projecting a deflationary period, and therefore is sending a signal in contradiction to what is expected from the market. These are the signals that result in the misallocation of resources in an economy not without consequences.

And how is the rate of interest related to that of profit? Equilibrium exists when the stock of capital is such that the rate of interest being determined by the level of savings is equal to the rate of profit controlled by the demand for output of capital. So, when Central Banks manipulate interest rates by keeping them below market levels, for the rate of profit to return to equilibrium, the cost of the capital stock must increase. This is known as a stock or asset bubble, a phenomenon of lowering interest rates below market levels. To demonstrate, let's say that the rates of interest and profit were in equilibrium at 5%. The owner of $100 of stock would earn profits of $5. Then the *Fed* lowers the interest rate to 3%. For the rate of profit to drop to 3%, and for the stock owner to maintain a profit of $5, the price of the stock would have to increase to $166.67, or a two-thirds increase. Stock owners feel enriched from this artificial increase and could realize these monetary benefits in the same way some benefit from Ponzi schemes.

Similar for real estate. As the mortgage rate drops, the prospective cost of the property increases. That's because the buyer's budget constraint in paying interest and repaying the loan doesn't change with the decrease in the interest rate, and savings from the lower interest rate could support a higher repayment on the loan. So potential homebuyers would bid the price of the property up until its budget constraint is attained. That is the new value of the home. The bottom line is lowering interest rates below market levels will invariably result in asset bubbles from the Cantillon effect and from the tendency of market forces to bring equilibrium back to parameter relationships.

IV (G) – GROSS DOMESTIC PRODUCT (*GDP*) AND OTHER MEASUREMENT PARAMETERS

"The welfare of a nation can scarcely be inferred from a measurement of national income."

Simon Kuznets, creator of GDP, 1962

Gross Domestic Product (GDP) is a monetary measurement of a country's economic output. When expressed in real terms, it provides a comparison of economic progress/development over time and when expressed on a basis of per-capita population, can be used to gauge productivity, prosperity, wealth, and wellbeing. There are weaknesses in the index such as the waste it may include as its formulations are not able to identify and factor out, its emphasis on material output ignores all the social and environmental costs it may be causing, and it offers no indication of the income and wealth disparities within a nation which could affect wellbeing.

In addition, comparing different countries' nominal *GDP*s for purposes of understanding the relative wellbeing of their populations can be misleading. Countries with high *GDP*s may also have high cost-of-living conditions and may not be better off than others with lower *GDP*s and cost-of-living indices. A better measure is the adjusted *GDP* for *Purchase Power Parity* (*PPP*) which takes cost-of-living conditions into consideration. For example, when applied to China's *GDP*, its *PPP* measured *GDP* is $10 trillion higher than its regular *GDP* in 2022.

GDP can be estimated by three approaches, all related. Since it represents the total economic output or production of a country, it can be computed by summing, according to the *US Bureau of Economic Analysis*, the Agency responsible for its development, *'the market value of all goods and services produced by labor and property within the United States.'* But workers are paid for their labor in wages, businesses earn profits, and lenders earn interest, so *GDP* value can also be determined by summing up the income of all the factors of production. And the third approach comes from the need of these income earners to spend their income on sustaining lives, lifestyles, on investments, and saving for future needs and contingencies. Technically, these three computations should produce identical estimates but would not, due to the robustness and reliability of data sources.

The measure of *GDP* has many limitations such as not accounting for negative externalities and non-monetary transactions, and wealth distribution, but perhaps its major weakness is its inability to adequately separate market prices from improvements in quality and/or decreases in quantity. For example, automobiles now contain features that were not present several years ago such as semi-autonomous driving capabilities. So, how much of the increase in their prices is due to this improvement and how much to the general rise in prices? Just as clueless consumers are to such a bifurcation, so is *GDP*. And recently, some manufacturers have been reducing package size yet charging the same package price as before the reduction. If *GDP* counts packages, it will overstate their value as there would now be more packages at the same price when production remained constant.

But there have been proposals to change the limitations in *GDP* and produce an index which more reflects the human condition and wellbeing. One such leading index is the *Human Development Index (HDI)* developed by Economist Mahbub ul Haq in 1990 for the *UN Development Program*. This index is a composite of three human conditions, life expectancy, years of education, and national income adjusted for cost-of-living or in *PPP* terms. Over time, the index is under constant improvement such as one for inequality *(IHDI)*. Nordic countries of Norway, Iceland, Finland, Denmark, and Sweden continue to dominate this index.

In the 2019 Report, of a total of 189 countries, the *US* was ranked 17th and 28th on the *HDI* and *IHDI* indices, respectively. China, with the second highest economy in terms of *GDP*, was ranked 85th on the *HDI* scale.

IV (H) – EMPLOYMENT

"In the past the man has been first; in the future the system must be first."
Frederick Winslow Taylor

Employment measures the participation of workers in an economy and the percentage of those participating who are employed or unemployed. It is perhaps the most important index monitored by policymakers as high unemployment rates are unlikely to raise approbation for their job approval and to increase chances for electability. The labor-force participation rate accounts for workers over age 16 with jobs or are actively seeking employment and excludes those in the armed forces and government institutions. In the *US*, as shown by the *BLS* chart, **Figure 11**, this rate has been decreasing gradually from 2002 when it peaked in that year at 66.776% to 62.169%, in July 2022, supposedly from the ageing of the working-age population. But there are also the disillusioned workers who are no longer seeking employment and whom Anne Case & Angus Deaton described in their book, *Deaths of Despair: And the Future of Capitalism*, as white and without a college education. The working population that previously found middle-class lifestyles from manufacturing jobs no longer do so because of offshoring and technological changes in the work process, and despair has set in. Many of these workers are no longer actively seeking employment and are thus not included in the rate.

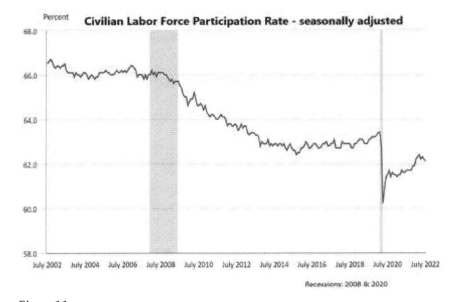

Figure 11

Source: **US Bureau of Labor Statistics**

But what useful information does this participation rate provide policy-makers? What does a declining rate mean? *The World Bank* estimates the labor participation rate globally at 64% in 2002 and 59% in 2021, two to three percentage points lower than the *US*. Is the *US* relatively better-off because of this? As shown in **Figure 11**, the participation rate decreases during recessions because many laid-off workers become discouraged and give up looking for jobs. They are supported by market restrictions and generous social benefit programs. But the *US* decline is not only driven by business cycles but rather there is growing evidence that more people are simply unable or unwilling to work at current wages. This became evident in 2021 and 2022 with worker shortages after the economy opened back from the pandemic restrictions, forcing employers to increase wage rates, and making a comeback for labor union representation. A couple instances of unions succeeding in unionizing their workers took place after the infamous votes at the Amazon warehouse on Staten Island and Starbucks in Buffalo, both located in New York. In these cases, policymakers take-away from declining participation rates is a shortage of labor with inflationary impacts on the economy.

Another takeaway is that the effects of the nonparticipation of labor will result in slower economic growth. A steadily shrinking participation rate means that fewer people are contributing to the production of goods and services, thus slowing the growth of *GDP*. In addition, many transfer and social security programs remain underfunded and depend on contributions from active workers. As this base decreases, the costs of these social programs are spread over fewer workers potentially increasing their tax liability or as is more likely from the response of the political class, increasing the public debt.

Another index monitored by policymakers is the unemployment rate, representing the percentage of active workers unable to find employment. In the *US* survey, if a worker is paid for work for at least one hour during the survey referenced week, that worker is considered employed. If a worker is not actively seeking employment anytime during the four-week period prior to, and including, the survey referenced week, the worker is not considered unemployed. So, with these restrictions in the formulation of the *US* unemployment rate, along with the labor participation rate, policymakers decide on what course of action to take on the economy.

In the *US*, restrictive measures to the labor market started in 1935 with its *National Labor Relations Act* that guarantees the right of private sector employees to organize into trade unions, engage in collective bargaining, and take collective action such as strikes. This was followed by the *Fair Labor Standards Act of 1939* which established a federal minimum wage provision, overtime pay, recordkeeping, and youth employment standards affecting employees throughout the economy. These Acts were implemented to diminish, if not eliminate, the movement towards *communism*, which had taken root in Eastern Europe.

Resulting from these market-determined restrictions, the hourly manufacturing wage rate started a rapid escalation from around 1979. In June 1979, the average wage rate for manufacturing was $6.56/hour (**Figure 12**). By July 2022, this had risen to $25.09/hour as shown on the *FRED* chart, an increase of 3.8 times despite significant job losses to offshoring and technological improvements over the same period. Manufacturing employment in the *US* decreased from 19.6 million in June 1979 to 12.8 million in July 2022, a loss of 6.8 million jobs (**Figure 13**).

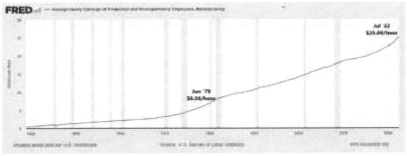

Figure 12

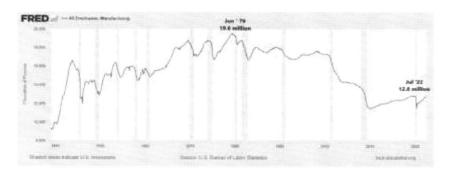

Figure 13

The fact is that *US* labor is over-priced compared to that of China, India, Mexico, and several other countries with similar skillsets, from its high cost-of-living occasioned by consumer price inflationary targets. Some federal bureaucracies understand this conundrum and for example, the minimum wage in 2022 has not changed since July 24, 2009, when it was established at the current level of $7.25 per hour. Increasing the *federal minimum wage* would cause a valid concern of labor attrition among those still earning that level of compensation, but these are a minority of workers as many states also have minimum wage laws which employers must comply with, and which provide greater employee so-called protections and minimum wages.

And not surprisingly, as *US* labor rates became uncompetitive, jobs relocated to states with right-to-work laws created under the *Taft-Hartley Act (The Labor Management Relations Act)*, which allow states to prohibit compulsory membership in a union, or these jobs simply moved to other countries. **Figure 14** shows the steep decline in union membership since 1983 when the *USBLS* started keeping comparable union data. Total membership in 2021 is about half it was in 1983 and the decline in the private sector union membership is more dramatic because those jobs are fungible compared to those in the public sector. So, jobs at the Pentagon cannot be readily moved to Mexico and there-fore cannot escape the inefficiencies associated with union membership.

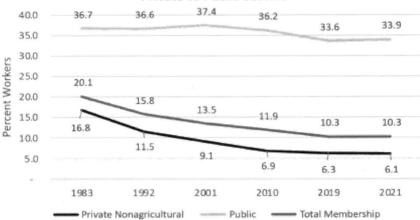

Figure 14

Source: US Bureau of Labor Statistics

One-third of these workers are union members versus one-eighteenth in the private sector. The public sector unions such as those representing teachers, police, and firemen, have significant political clout and an endorsement of a candidate, can affect the outcome of an election and in turn, safeguard/promote the interests of the unions. As union members can earn as much as 30% in higher pay than a comparable non-union worker, these inefficiencies are only adding to the country's high cost-of- living, deficits, and debts, which obligations future generations will have to address without having received the benefits.

And as with all goods that are overpriced, demand for labor is curtailed. Before, labor commanded employment contracts with generous benefits including paid vacations and time off for illness, pension contributions, training, life and medical insurances, etc., but now wage rates are trending towards market levels. This is terrible news in a high cost-of-living economy. Consequently, more are living paycheck to paycheck, utilizing social food programs and food donations banks while actively working, living in their cars again while holding down a job and working multiple jobs to make ends meet. A new economy has popped up known as the gig economy, an online platform for labor services usually on a piecemeal, short-term basis, where workers are considered self-employed and are therefore denied employee benefits. The gig economy, which some estimates put as high as 30% of *US* employment and growing, is a market-driven system as compared to a unionized system for labor services. The natural reaction to the falling welfare of workers is to blame employers for their exploitation not the irresponsible politicians who caused the mess.

V

COMPONENTS OF ECONOMIC DESTRUCTION

THIS SECTION DISCUSSES the components that comprise the political economy that can be manipulated to serve special interests at the cost of delayed economic destruction. By far, the component with the most destructive power when misused and abused is a country's use of fiat currency, a currency without any intrinsic value. Its value comes from the acceptance by users, sometimes irrational, that someone else is willing to take it for the nominal value stated on its face. When that bond is broken, there are serious consequences for the economy of the country whose currency was rejected.

But other components can also be quite damaging. *The National Income Index, GDP,* which is falsely portrayed to give a sense of well-being, can be increased by population growth and deficit spending; inflation targets allow central banks to increase the money supply while increasing the cost-of-living and labor costs; cutting business- and household-tax obligations without spending reductions increase public deficits and debts; and money printing known as *Quantitative Easing* will only inflate asset prices such as real estate and stocks. The impacts of these abuses will continue to be delayed as long as possible but for the *US* and other developed countries, time has run out. The liberal order governing their conduct is being challenged by the despair of the working class with reactions of civil unrest, nativism, and self-inflicted harm.

V (A) – FIAT CURRENCY

Fiat currency in the form of paper has been around in China since the Yuan Dynasty, 13th century CE and even before then, but did not become universally accepted until *US* president, Richard Nixon, decoupled the *US* dollar from gold in 1971. Prior to this time and after 1944, gold was redeemable for *US* dollars by foreign governments under conditions established by the *Bretton Woods Agreement*. But 1971 was the year that countries embarked on a currency with no intrinsic value, although as money it is expected to have the attribute of being a store of value. Its value lies in its government designating it legal tender and its acceptance as such by the financial establishment.

As fiat is inconvertible and cannot be redeemed since there is no underlying commodity/assets backing it, the currency is at the whims of the government. This comes about because fiat currency need not be scarce and can be readily manufactured at a fraction of its face-value cost. Central banks, therefore, have greater control over its supply, which allows for the limited management of financial variables such as credit supply, liquidity, interest rates, and money velocity. Limited because trying to manage these financial variables does not always achieve desired results as was the case during the financial crisis of 2007. But there are more opportunities for destruction from the creation of bubbles due to its unlimited supply.

Supporters of fiat currency usually cite a few reasons for its justification. One is that governments demand payment of taxes in the fiat currency it issues, which, since taxes payments are applicable to everyone, should make it acceptable to everyone. As an extension of this case, money is but an *IOU* from the State and it recovers its *IOUs* through obligations of payments to governments such as taxes, fees, and penalties. Another justification put forward is the credit theory of money which holds that money doesn't have to have intrinsic value since it's equivalent to debt. The primary purpose of money is to act as a *unit of account*, to denominate debt. So, a debtor would be funded by a creditor or bank with the obligation of repayment in the same monetary unit.

Figure 15

Source: **World Bank**

Figure 15a

Source: **World Bank**

But these are flimsy justifications. They don't have built-in mechanisms for self-discipline. Any commodity that can be easily and inexpensively reproduced and the reproduction of which can be used to inveigle opinions on communal benefits, despite the longer-term destructive effects, will need to be curtailed. Politicians don't have this self-discipline and promote unsupported money expansion as a means to electability and serving self-interests.

But currencies without intrinsic value, when abused because it's easy to do so, are inflationary, and depending on the level of abuse, can be hyperinflationary, greatly reducing the purchasing power of those currencies. The charts, shown as **Figures 15 & 16**, demonstrate this principle as they compare some countries which currencies have recently shown significant depreciation from government policies of increasing their money supply.

Nigeria has experienced double-digit inflation between 2016 and 2020 with attendant high increases to its money supply. This is despite the country being the largest oil and gas producer in Africa with reserves of 37 billion barrels. Were it not in this position, it would certainly be in a hyperinflationary situation from that level of monetary stimulation. Sudan, a country lacking the export potential of Nigeria would not fare as

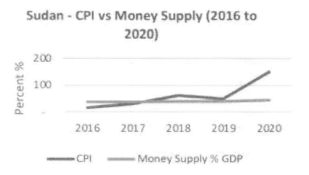

Figure 16

Source: **World Bank**

Figure 16a

Source: **World Bank**

well and as shown, with similar monetary expansion did have significant currency depreciation in the period (**Figures 16 & 16a**).

Interestingly, the European Union, with similar monetary stimulus, has extremely low inflationary pressures during the same period. The difference is the European Union's advanced capital markets act as a sponge sucking the rise in prices towards the asset classes. The *US* expansion would show similar impacts on *CPI* from monetary expansion as the European Union because of the same reasoning, a highly developed capital market.

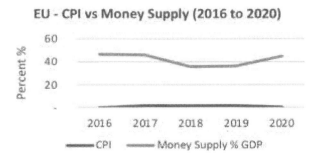

Figure 17

Source: **World Bank**

Figure 17a

Source: **World Bank**

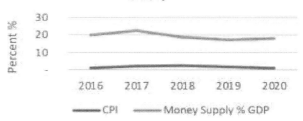

Figure 18

Source: **World Bank**

Figure 18a

Source: **World Bank**

V (B) – DESTRUCTION, *GDP* GROWTH

For the reason it is seen as an index of economic progress, *GDP* has been hijacked by the political class to be used and abused for its self-interests. If *GDP* growth is seen as an important measure of national and economic success, and it can be managed/manipulated, it could become an important tool for those that benefit from such perceptions. This is accomplished by enticing more people to consume their future income, or incur debt, and for the rapid escalation of public debt not only in the *US* but worldwide. Countries are drowning in public debt which can never and will never be repaid for the sole purpose of increasing the growth in *GDP*. **Figure 19** shows public debt keeping pace with *GDP* over the past decade and is almost equivalent for most of that period, except the pandemic years where increases in debt were mitigating factors for the hit to *GDP* from economic restrictions and lockdowns. And this would be expected as public debt is a component of *GDP* and changes in it would lead to changes in *GDP* unless offset by other factors.

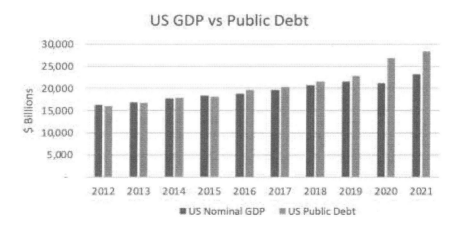

Figure 19

Source: Federal Reserve Economic Data (FRED)

The political elites would even go to great lengths to prevent corrective action when their monetary policies cause the potential for destructive conditions to the economy that must be addressed. Inducing a recession is a natural corrective measure to rapid and inflationary growth of an economy, but this is never tolerated by countries as they engage in half-measures they refer to as a *"Soft Landing"* with the intent of continuing to push the problem further into the future.

World Population vs *GDP* Growth 2012 to 2021

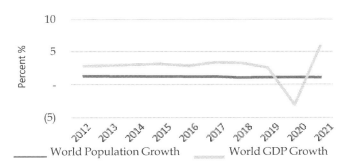

World Population Growth   World GDP Growth

Figure 20

Source: **World Bank**

US Population vs *GDP* Growth 2012 to 2021

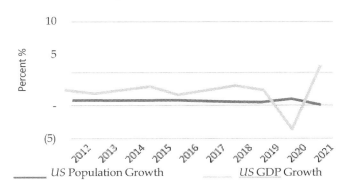

US Population Growth   *US* GDP Growth

Figure 21

Source: **World Bank**

Another factor leading to growth in *GDP* is population growth. As population increases, there is additional demand for goods and services that would not have existed were it not for the increase, thus growing *GDP*. In 1970, the World population was 3.7 billion and 50 years later, 7.8 billion, more than doubling. And it is known that such unsustainable population growth is causing Malthusian outcomes, which causation is deflected from too many people to too much carbon being released in the atmosphere. Therefore, no country is addressing the problem apart from China with its one-child-per-family policy which it has now modified, with the justification of worker shortages. As addressing the harm of population growth would have consequences for the electability of the political class, it rarely becomes a topic for discussion. **Figures 20 and 21** show the close correlation between population growth and that of *GDP*. The world population and its *GDP* during the past decade, 2012 to 2021, has been increasing at about 1% and 3% per annum, respectively, except for the pandemic years. The relationship is similar for the *US*.

V (C) – INFLATION TARGETS

The *Fed* has been using an annual inflation target of 2%, as measured by the price index for personal consumption expenditures, since 2012, and has justified it as being most consistent with its mandate for maximum employment and price stability. It goes about meeting this target through its *Open Market Operations*, ultimately resulting in money supply changes. As it became shackled by inflation exceeding the 2% annual level, which would have curbed it money supply expansion, in 2020, the *Fed* modified the annual target to a longer period based on averaging as in some years, the rate of inflation was below 2% target. So, if after say 4 years, the average rate of inflation was 1.5%, the *Fed* felt that the economy could tolerate a higher rate in the fifth and successive years, which would result in an average of 2% over a longer period, and in this case the 5th year would have a target of 4%. One of the concerns expressed by the

Fed is, as inflation expectations fall due to low rates of inflation, interest rates would also decrease, limiting its response to an economic downturn requiring monetary stimulation.

The *Fed* justification for the 2% target is quite baffling since it hardly achieves the target and thus unable to accurately gauge its effect on employment and price stability. Over the last 10 years, it has undershot the target in 6 of those and exceeded it in the remaining 4 years. The fact is that any inflation is destructive to an economy and must be minimized at all costs. As pointed out before, the 2% target, now adopted by the developed countries, was arbitrarily selected, and has no basis for its use. It has been in use in some countries since the 1990s. The fact that even at 2% per annum, the cost-of-living doubles every 35 years makes it not surprising that countries that have been using this target the longest also have some of the highest cost-of-living indices. The table (**Figure 22**) clearly demonstrates this phenomenon. Inflation targeting started in the early 1990s in New Zealand and adopted by several countries during that time, including Canada and the United Kingdom. The *US* officially came on board in 2012. Using the *US* cost-of-living as a base (=100), relative indices can be expressed for all other countries in the population being ranked/compared, which for this exercise is 107 countries. Those countries pioneering inflation targets back in the 1990s have some of the highest cost-of-living indices in the World. For example, in Bermuda, a *UK* oversees territory, the cost-of-living is 57.6% higher than that of the *US* and it is deemed to have the highest cost-of-living. Israel is number 4 ranked, while New Zealand is at 13. The problem with a country's high cost-of-living is its effect on wages, which need to keep up to allow people to meet their wants and needs. If each country was an island economy cut off from the rest of the world in trade, high cost-of-living and high wages wouldn't matter. But the reality is that capital flows to where it maximizes its returns and high wages will not attract capital or production. Workers in these high-wage countries have become uncompetitive

Effects on Cost of Living from Inflation Targets 10 Countries Pioneering Targets				
Country	Inflation Target Date Implemented	Inflation Target %	Cost-of-Living Index (US = 100)	Cost-of-Living Rank (107 Countries)
New Zealand	12/1989	0%–2% & 0%–3% (since 1996)	117.2	13
	02/1991	1%–3% (2% mid-range)	105.6	18
Canada	02/1991	1%–3% (2% mid-range)	105.6	18
United Kingdom	10/1992	2%	107.9	17
Bermuda (UK Territory)	10/1992	2%	157.6	1
Cayman Islands (UK Territory)	10/1992	2%	137.9	3
Turks & Caicos Islands (UK Territory)	10/1992	2%	124.6	7
Sweden	01/1993	2% starting in 1995 with +/– 1% tolerance	109.3	15
Australia	06/1993	2%–3%	118.0	12
Israel	06/1997	1%–3% (since 2003)	130.2	4
Iceland	03/2001	2%	128.0	5
United States	01/2012	2%	100.0	20

Figure 22

Source: WorldData

and redundant. It is the situation throughout the *US* and Europe as off-shoring of manufacturing jobs and technology for jobs substitution of all others are leading to the despair workers are experiencing and the resulting irrational actions being taken.

Not surprisingly, some of these high cost-of-living countries will have negative *current account trade balances (CABs)* as their exports have been curtailed by their inability to be competitive. The *US* leads in this regard although it is the 20th ranked cost-of-living country. But it imports far more only because it can due to its reserve currency status. The country can create money to pay for its net imports whereas most countries would face deterioration in their currencies if they were running negative *CABs*. Exporting countries to the *US*, such as China, accepts the *US* currency in exchange for goods and services. This is a good deal for the *US* as it receives production representing value in exchange for dollars with no intrinsic value. The table at **Figure 23** shows correlation of some of the large economies in North America and Europe with high cost-of-livings to negative *CABs*, presumably due to their uncompetitive situation curtailing their ability to increase exports.

High Cost-of-living Indices vs Current Account Balances (CAB) 5 Countries with High CoL & Deficit CAB				
Country	*Cost-of-Living Index*	*Cost-of-living Rank*	*CAB Deficit billion US$ (2019)*	*CAB Deficit Rank*
United States	100	20	–480.2	1
United Kingdom	107.7	17	–121.9	2
Ireland	119.8	11	–45.0	5
Canada	105.6	18	–35.4	6
France	96.2	23	–18.1	10

Figure 23

Source: US Trade Representative & World Data

So, it is quite apparent that inflation targeting, even at the low level of 2%, will increase a country's cost-of-living, and over time lead to over-priced labor rates, uncompetitive outputs, deficit current account trade balances, and currency depreciation, all undesirable outcomes for an economy. But is encouraged by the political class and cohorts as it serves to prop up nominal *GDP*, facilitates the servicing of debt (repayment is cheaper dollars), which gives a false sense of wellbeing.

V (D) – DEFICIT-CAUSING TAX CUTS

Modern tax cuts started during the Reagan administration in 1981. In that year, *US* President Ronald Reagan and his supporters pushed tax reform by passing *The Economic Recovery Tax Act of 1981*, and later in his administration, *The Tax Reform Act of 1986*. The objective was a general reduction in the personal income tax and capital gains tax rates, and although during this eight-year administration there were decreases and increases in these tax rates, the net effect was that the highest personal tax rate decreased from about 70% to 28%, and the capital gains tax settled also at 28%.

But this administration saw no need to reduce government spending corresponding to the reduced revenues from the tax cuts. Instead, public expenditures were increased, primarily the Department of Defense, and the *US* became the nation having the largest public debt. During the eight years between 1981 and 1989, the *US* national debt increased from $997.8 billion in 1981 to $2.9 trillion by 1989, or by $1.9 trillion (because of the overlap of budgets and administrations, although Reagan would have taken office in 1980, his first budget would not have had an influence until the following year).

So, the administration embarked on a popular political strategy by combining ideology (smaller government, lower tax rates) with deficit spending, which expands the economy and give people the false feeling of improved wellbeing. This was done to continue popularity and serve the political self-interests of the Republican Party. Tax cuts combined with deficit spending, got Ronald Reagan elected for his maximum two terms and has been the mantra of his party since then. This was echoed by Vice-President, Dick Cheney in 2002 when he said that *"Reagan proved that deficits don't matter, we won the mid-terms. This is our due."* VP Cheney was expressing the strategy of the then President, George W. Bush.

But before George W. Bush was his father, George H. W. Bush, the Vice President in the Ronald Reagan administration. President Bush is the only Republican since Reagan not supportive of tax cuts as a strategy for growing the economy, referred to as supply-side economics and which Bush had described as *"voodoo economics"* during his primary debates with Reagan. He was elected President in 1988 and during his administration, practiced what he believed in and raised taxes on higher earners to reduce the Reagan budget deficits. But he paid the price as he became a one-term president having broken a campaign promise of not raising taxes, and by so doing, lost the support of conservative Republicans. Thus, George H. W. Bush was one of the few politicians for whom taking a principled position on reducing budget deficits was more expedient to being re-elected.

George H. W. Bush was replaced by Democratic President, Bill Clinton. The Democratic Party was not committed to smaller government as were the Republicans and certainly not to tax cuts. So, during the Clinton administration, two Acts, the *Omnibus Budget Reconciliation Act of 1993* and the *Balanced Budget Act of 1997* were passed with the focus of reducing budget deficits through tax increases on the wealthiest taxpayers and on corporate income, and through spending cuts. This was accomplished by creating new income brackets, increasing the top federal tax rate from 31% to 39.6%, increasing the highest corporate tax rate from 34% to 38%, setting limits on itemized deductions, and implementing $255 billion in spending cuts mainly affecting Medicare and the military budgets.

These measures resulted in budget surpluses starting in 1998. But despite these efforts at deficit reduction, and which produced desirable results towards the end, the national debt grew by $1.4 trillion during the Clinton's administration.

Bill Clinton was succeeded by George W. Bush who did not share the principled approach of his father to fiscal responsibility and quickly adopted the Reagan approach of tax cutting and deficit spending. His father had moved in the other direction and paid the price of being a single term president. George W. was not going to make the same mistake especially when there was a model to successfully becoming a two-term president, put into effect by Ronald Reagan. So, the George W. Bush administration crafted and passed two major pieces of tax-cut legislation, the *Economic Growth and Tax Relief Reconciliation Act of 2001 (EGTRRA)*, and the *Jobs and Growth Tax Relief Reconciliation Act of 2003 (JGTRRA)*. These Acts initiated tax rebates, created new tax brackets with lower tax rates, lowered Clinton's 39.6% tax rate for the highest tax bracket to 35%, introduced sweeping changes to retirement plans, increased the child tax credit, and decreased the capital gains tax rates among other measures.

From a budget surplus, the non-partisan *Congressional Budget Office (CBO)*, estimated that the Bush tax cuts added $1.5 trillion to the national debt, excluding interest, over the decade ending 2011. But the administration was faced with other issues such as the war on terror and resorted to funding these initiatives with debt. The increase in debt during the Bush administration ballooned to $5.85 trillion between 2002 and 2009. The *"deficits don't matter"* mantra was being tested.

President Barack Obama succeeded George W. Bush and had campaigned on maintaining the Bush tax cuts for the lower and middle-class families. But by the mid-term congressional elections, the Democrats had lost their majorities in both chambers, which had given the Country *"Obamacare"* health care improvements, and the Republican majorities were not supportive of increasing taxes on the rich. The Bush tax cuts had an expiry date and unless acted upon, would have reverted to tax rates existing before the reductions. The Obama administration reached a compromise with the congressional leaders basically to extend the Bush tax cuts for an additional two years and there was some money thrown in for unemployment insurance and payroll tax cuts. This was incorporated in the *Tax Relief, Unemployment Insurance Reauthorization, and Job Creation Act of 2010,* and through another compromise most of these tax cuts were made permanent in the *American Taxpayer Relief Act of 2012.*

As the Obama administration dealt with the continuing war on terror, the great financial recession of 2008, health care reform, and incorporation of the Bush tax cuts, all funded by debt, it is therefore not surprising that the national debt under his administration was higher than any previous administration, at $8.6 trillion during the eight years 2009 to 2017. The total national debt in 2017 was $20.2 trillion, an incredible level and over 20 times that at the start of the Reagan administration, which Americans used to consider troubling.

The Donald Trump administration followed and quickly set about passing the *Tax Cuts and Jobs Act of 2017* that, in the republican tradition, reduced taxes on individuals and businesses, limited deductions, and eliminated the alternative minimum tax for corporations. While the corporation tax cuts were permanent, many of the income tax cut provisions will expire in 2025. The *CBO* estimates that the Trump tax cuts would add $2.3 trillion to the national debt over a 10-year period. President Trump's single term in office, 2018 to 2021, added $6.7 trillion to the national debt for a total of $26.9 trillion, mainly from pandemic restrictions and relief payments.

President Biden's administration, a democratic one, took office in 2021 and continued the pandemic relief and stimulus measures of the Trump administration, and funded an infrastructural bill, with a total debt impact of $2.3 trillion over ten years. But the debt keeps growing and by year 2023, it stood above $32 trillion or approximately $95,000 per capita. A debt jubilee seems to be in the making for creditors. A jubilee, meaning forgiveness, may have already started with President Biden's failed proposal to forgive a portion of student debt[13], but unlike national debt, creditors will not be burdened by this jubilee.

The bottom line is that politicians in the *US*, since the Reagan administration and more so from the republican party, except for the principled George H. W. Bush, have been approving deficit budgets due to unfunded tax cuts, consequently growing the national debt, and postponing the consequences to future generations. Budget deficits help their re-election efforts and thus the special interests they represent. Their apologists rationalize low interest rates for the larger amount of debt – the demand curve of lower prices leading to increased consumption – conveniently forgetting that the price of debt is not market-determined but is established by the manipulation of the money supply by the central planners. Debt is the Achilles heel of any economy and the reason some are evading this vulnerability is the irrational acceptance of some currencies, it's the difference in acceptability of the peso in Argentina, and the yen in Japan or the dollar in the *US*. Argentina's national debt to *GDP* ratio in 2022 was 78.6% whereas Japan's, one of the highest in the World, was 266% and the *US*, 136%, yet Argentina has a hyperinflation rate of 71% in July 2022 compared to 2.6% in Japan and 8.5% in the *US*.

---

13 A legal challenge at the *US Supreme Court* led to the rejection of the proposal but has since been replaced by an income-based repayment program with a balance-forgiveness terminal time frame. This new approach is expected to add $127 billion to public debt (NYT, November 10, 2023, 'How Millions of Borrowers Got $127 billion in Student Loans Canceled')

VI

SYMPTOMS OF ECONOMIC DESTRUCTION

THIS SECTION DEALS with phenomena that can be associated with an economy's pending destruction and which main events the author calls "*the four horsemen of the apocalypse*". Some, such as environmental degradation may be outside the control of a nation, but others are clearly of its making. Debt, inflation, and wealth inequality are controllable and unless the nation is an island economy, meaning it's cut off from the rest of the world, failure to do so will induce global sanctions in the form of currency debasement and uncompetitive production. The nation is then left in strife, with its people seeking relief in migration to better functioning countries or turning inwards with nativistic policies and those rejecting global solutions. This condition is characterized by despair among its people as being witnessed currently in the *US* and Western Europe. As a consequence, some of these countries have elected governments with nativist/xenophobic and deglobalization agendas, enforced through stricter border regulation, trade barriers, and buy-local campaigns. These "solutions" do not address the root cause of the problem, high cost of living and uncompetitive wage rates, and are destined to fail, with the potential of escalating the failed solutions to conflict as currently being witnessed by the tensions in the relationship between the *US* and China.

VI (A) – UNCOMPETITIVE LABOR

In today's economies, labor must be skilled and competitive. Countries with labor forces that meet these two conditions, as several Asian countries do, perform particularly well in employment, production and ultimately, global distribution. The *US* and Europe, having some of the best universities worldwide, are not deficient with this requirement. Most of the talent in Asia got their start at these universities and these Western Universities still depend on this clientele for a sizable part of its revenues. The *US* and Europe fail with the competitive requirements because they are high cost-of-living countries. As can be seen in the table, **Figure 24**, of the thirty countries with the highest cost-of-living indices, it is dominated by European countries and includes the *US* at number 20th. Even some of the countries listed that are not located in Europe, such as Bermuda, Cayman Islands and Turks & Caicos, are self-governing territories of the *UK*, a European country.

These countries can be expected to have high labor rates, an inducement for manufacturing to go offshore or become capital-intensive to remain viable. Jobs that cannot move, mainly in the public and service sectors, are being replaced by technology or being transferred to the customer. Long gone are full service gas stations replaced by self-service ones; customers must now check-in and tag their luggage at airports; they also interact with a machine which compares their passport photos to their images before sending them along to an immigration officer; check-out at some retail stores is accomplished without human intervention; many are no longer accepting cash as payment as that may require the provision of change, a time-consuming task; banks in Sweden charge a fee for cash deposits as cash requires costly storage areas at the banks; travel directions are now given by holograms which look human at first glance; and face recognition software is helping to solve crimes and in China, to force compliance with social expectations.

Thirty Highest Cost-of-Living Countries					
Country Rank	Country	CoL Index	Country Rank	Country	CoL Index
1	Bermuda	157.6	16	Finland	108.0
2	Switzerland	142.4	17	United Kingdom	107.9
3	Cayman Islands	137.9	18	Canada	105.6
4	Israel	130.2	19	Japan	101.9
5	Iceland	128.0	20	United States	100.0
6	New Caledonia	125.8	21	Netherlands	99.0
7	Turks & Caicos	124.6	22	Belgium	97.0
8	Norway	124.6	23	France	96.2
9	Barbados	121.5	24	Austria	95.9
10	Denmark	119.9	25	Germany	92.3
11	Ireland	119.8	26	South Korea	87.0
12	Australia	118.0	27	Italy	86.2
13	New Zealand	117.2	28	Spain	82.9
14	Luxembourg	113.1	29	Hong Kong	77.9
15	Sweden	109.3	30	Portugal	76.4

Figure 24   Source: OECD, World Bank, IMF & Eurostat

And the technologies planned are more daunting. Oxford University predicted that 47% of jobs in the *US* existing in 2013 will disappear by around 2030. There will be new jobs created but not at the level of those lost. Soon, autonomous vehicles, computers on wheels, will be self-operating and can be summoned quickly by a click of an app on a smart phone. Since the purpose of vehicles is to provide transportation, there would be no need to own a car. Trucks will no longer need drivers. The entire automotive industry will be in turmoil as fewer vehicles are needed. Your car is on call at your fingertips and for a fraction of the cost to own it. And if cars and trucks can self-operate safely, who needs auto insurance? Packages will be delivered more expeditiously by drones, further removing the need for truck drivers. 3-D

Printing will eliminate the need to visit the retail store for most non-food items. They are already building large multistoried structures. The retail sector, seemingly in a push for wage increases, will not be spared, and automation is already taking hold. There is a new coffee franchise in New York, *Blank Street Coffee*, that operates its stores with two employees. And not only blue-collar jobs are at risk. There are already neural-learning algorithms that can write articles on subjects better and faster than the journalists who wrote them before, perform better at medical diagnosing than medical doctors, and perform legal research faster than any paralegal can. As this is being written, *ChatGPT*, a new generative AI platform from OpenAI, is causing media waves for its capabilities to analyze and understand customer queries and carry on a human-like conversation. This is the future in which labor will be almost absent in the production process. To understand how vulnerable labor is in the developed countries, a case in 2016 at *Foxconn*, is revealing. *Foxconn*, a Taiwanese electronic Company which makes components for Apple, laid off 60,000 workers, replaced by technology. What was notable about this retrenchment was not the magnitude of it but the average wage of those whose jobs were replaced. It was *US*$5 per day. So, if you work for *US*$5 per day or more, your job is on the line. This seems to have bypassed the political elite, some of whom are actively advocating increasing the federal minimum wage in the *US* from $7.25 to $15 per hour. Proposals such as this will put more workers on the breadline as Employers fast-track some of the technologies described above to replace them or shift their jobs overseas.

Labor is becoming irrelevant because it's overpriced in many countries. To expand, a commodity is overpriced when it can readily be replaced by cheaper alternatives such as, in the case of labor, technology and/or outsourcing to lower-priced regions and countries. American workers don't add enough value to commodities produced, or to their numbers (known as productivity), to justify the difference in their compensation. American workers in the manufacturing sector earn six times more than workers in Mexico, nine times more than those in China and a whooping 24 times more than those in India. As with all products that are overpriced, their demand declines until they become expendable. This is the case with workers in most of the world as demonstrated by the Foxconn example.

The American worker, sensing his lack of relevance in the emerging world order, is anxious and fearful. Although the changes will start in those countries with the highest wage structures, it's only a matter of time before it trickles down to middle-income countries unless politicians stop this madness of intervening and placing restrictions on the labor market. Workers in developed countries, and where these labor restrictions are not working, are starting to employ market-driven solutions. The fastest growing employment in the *US* is gig work, work done outside the realm of an employee contract and without the associated benefits. Workers are using gig work primarily to supplement income from regular employment or to take advantage of the flexibility it offers. But politicians can't leave well-enough-alone as there is a push on their part to reclassify these jobs from a self-employment status to one of regular employment requiring the employer to be liable for employee benefits. The rate of growth of these jobs will depend on how successful these Machiavellians are at their destructive scheme.

As desperation among workers grows, illiberal solutions are starting to take hold, especially in the developed countries. These involve the rejection of globalization and all the comparable advantages accompanying that, applying restrictions to foreign produced goods primarily through the application of duties, and reshoring — bowing to political pressure to return production to the high cost developed countries, or rationalizing it on just-in-case rather than just-in-time supply chain phenomenon. All these measures only serve to further exacerbate the high cost-of-living in these countries, making workers more expendable, and desperation and conflict more likely.

And then there are the laws that tie the hands of employers with respect to replacing employees, the major one being age discrimination. There was a time when it was felt that attaining the age of 65 was the age workers' contributions peaked and thereafter started to decline. It is known that as one gets older, energy levels and brain capacity decrease after a certain age. This is all tied into the life span of humans. And in past times, workers were expected to, and did as company policy, retire from company employment. No longer. Workers can now be seen occupying jobs well into their 80s and beyond the average life cycle of the country. These workers can't be as productive as younger ones, but employers continue to hire to avoid the risks associated with applying age discrimination. It's not that there are no volunteer jobs, or self-employment for those who wish to continue working, the problem is that by continuing to fill paid positions, they are blocking the employment of younger workers. The New York Times, in its May 5, 2023 Editorial, dealt with the harm to legislation and appointments Dianne Feinstein, a Senator from California, who is 89 years old and unable, because of age-related health problems, to attend legislative sessions, was causing.[14] The Editorial concluded that "Senate seats are not lifetime sinecures." But that is true of all institutional jobs, public or private, where individuals are unable to perform in a competitive mode and therefore should not be allowed to occupy those positions. The decision should not be left to the worker, as in the case of Ms. Feinstein, as greed and selfishness are often behind their decision to continue working. The Country needs legislation that sets a cap on employable age, whether 65, 70 or whatever it considers appropriate. If a Company considers a worker to be indispensable, it can always retain its service under a consultant contract. But no one should have the right to work past their productive years at their volition, supported by the certainty of a favorable age-discrimination court ruling.

14 Ms. Feinstein died on September 29, 2023, at age 90.

So, developed countries basically have high cost-of-living attributes and thus over-priced labor from targeting what they consider to be a modest level of inflation. If allowed to function, the market will correct for this condition but at a cost. Countries with high cost-of-living which cannot sell their goods and services on the global market, will experience a decline in the value of their currencies from a fall-off in demand. Although inflationary to those populations as importers would need more local currency to pay for imports, exports become cheaper due to the converse argument of importing countries needing less of their currency to pay for exports from the high cost-of-living countries. The relative values of the foreign exchange among currencies would bring about the necessary equilibrium that would eliminate the need for the illiberal solutions taking hold in these developed countries. Uncompetitive labor-forces in high cost-of-living countries are destructive to their economies but as the pain from corrective action is counter-intuitive to the interest of the policy makers, it will continue being postponed. Inflation in asset prices will continue to be spun as investors' confidence in the economy, and general inflation continues to undergo definitional changes to mask its magnitude. But postponement makes the situation more dire with larger deficit trade balances, increased public and private debt, illiberal policies, and social unrest.

VI (B) – ENVIRONMENTAL DEGRADATION

Besides the financial consequences of unsustainable debt, the societal/ social cost to increasing *GDP* is hardly ever recognized and never acted upon. The primary question here is can the world population satisfy its insatiable needs and wants from a finite resource base in a sustainable way? The answer is an obvious and resounding NO. But delays of the inevitable are possible through increased material productivity, and population reduction.

Our planet is warming. *NASA* reported that "eighteen of the nineteen warmest years all have occurred since 2001."[15] Further, Carl Zimmer, in a recent New York Times article[16], reported that the concentration in our atmosphere of carbon dioxide, one of the gasses causing the temperature changes, is 410 parts per million, a level not seen at least for the last 3 million years. And if this is not already distressing, the Russian perma-frost, which trapped vast amounts of carbon dioxide, is starting to melt releasing its trapped greenhouse gas.

The effects of all this carbon are starting to take hold. The United Nations reported that cyclone Idai which hit Southeastern Africa in March 2019, was the worst weather disaster to ever strike the Southern Hemisphere. Ever! We know what happens when the Planet cools — ice forms at and around its poles, but we have no experience when it changes course. But we can surmise quite accurately what will happen as ice melts, sea levels rise, and ocean temperatures increase. More Idais, destruction, misery, and death. And certainly, more *evers*.

The costs of these changes are enormous. At the World Economic Forum's annual meeting at Davos, Switzerland on 23 May 2022, a new report from the *Deloitte Center for Sustainable Progress (DCSP)* estimated that, if left unchecked, climate change could cost the global economy *US$178* trillion over the next 50 years, or a 7.6% cut to global *gross domestic product (GDP)* in the year 2070 alone. In the *US*, the White House Office of Management & Budget, based on current warming trends, predicted climate change could reduce the country's *Gross Domestic Product*, or economic output, by as much as 10% by the end of this century.

Climate change is wiping out wealth. But the World is focused on reducing human-produced greenhouse gases which are held responsible

15 Global Temperature: LATEST ANNUAL AVERAGE ANOMALY, 2018, article updated annually at https://climate.nasa.gov/vital-signs/global-temperature/.
16 The Lost History of One of the World's Strangest Science Experiments, March 29, 2019; https://www.nytimes.com/2019/03/29/sunday-review/biosphere-2-climate-change.html

for these changes. In that same report, *DCSP* concentrated on four key stages for decarbonization globally. This attention is misdirected as greenhouse gases are just symptomatic of the real problem, the planet's over-population by humans. Fifty years ago, the world's population was 3 billion. In 2022, it stands at 7.3 billion, a 143% increase. It can be hypothesized that this rapid increase was partly due to the era of monetary expansion from the adoption of fiat currency, which gave a false sense of security. Climate change is a corrective mechanism to return the Earth's equilibrium.

Thomas Robert Malthus, an English Philosopher in the eighteen/nineteen centuries, postulated that in a period of resource abundance, a population would grow rapidly, but as the margin of abundance could not be sustained, checks on population growth, including famine, disease, and wars, would reduce those levels back to those that are supportable. To avoid such a catastrophe, Malthus urged controls on population growth. To rephrase, Malthus theory is that the World could sustain a given level of population and it self-corrects when exceeded. Currently there is a superbug, Candida Auris, sweeping the World for which there is no cure. It has reported to have killed over 700,000 people and its origins are unknown. The World Health Organization estimated that approximately 7 million people have died globally from the *COVID* virus which is still infecting people. These are a couple of Malthus' corrective measures just as climate change threatens food production and living conditions with drought, floods, storms, and fires. Climate change is directly related to overpopulation.

And as living conditions worsen, it has spawned large movements of migrants and asylum seekers to the developed neighboring countries. It goes without saying that this is only the beginning of the crisis, because the conditions inciting people to flee their homelands will only worsen. But the backlash has started. The election of an unsuited person to the presidency of the *US* and the apparent irrational decision of the British to leave the EU, are examples of the xenophobia gripping countries to which these immigrants are fleeing. But presidents should know that walls serve to keep people in on both sides.

Undoubtedly, climate change is man-made and directly attributed to world over-population. The main way to reverse it is population reduction. But as Malthus theorizes, the planet self-corrects. Obviously, seven to eight billion is not a sustainable level and storms, fires, floods, drought, famine, and wars will take their toll. Fears are justified.

In the *US* alone, droughts are removing farmlands from cultivation in Western states where the *US Drought Monitor* estimated that on July 11, 2022, 32% percent of the lands there were classified as experiencing extreme or exceptional drought. One of these States, California, leads the country in agricultural products accounting for nearly 11% of the national total, and drought is impacting its agriculture sector. To this, add the destruction of wildfires spurred by the dryness. Droughts not only reduce farm income, but the country's *GDP* and as supply is curtailed, general inflation rises.

The effects also apply to waterways in that part of the country such as the Colorado River, a 1,450-mile-long river which basin is in several Southwestern states including Arizona, California, Colorado, New Mexico, Nevada, Utah, and Wyoming. States such as Arizona and Nevada were being ordered to cut their water consumption from drought effects. Lake Mead, an artificial reservoir formed by the Hoover Dam hydro facility, was at 27% capacity in 2022, about 175 feet lower than in the year 2000. Further North, the Missouri River is also impacted by drought affecting several states including Nebraska, Iowa, Kansas, Minnesota, Missouri, Montana, North Dakota, South Dakota, and Wyoming. According to the *National Drought Mitigation Center*, in 2022, approximately 62% of the Missouri River basin is experiencing some form of abnormally dry or drought conditions, with 6% being extreme or exceptional drought. Falling water levels in major rivers would result in higher costs for transportation, energy — from hydro power or cooling of conventional generators, for cultivating farm products, and simply maintaining the population who depend on the river for its water consumption.

And then there are the floods from environmental degradation. During the summer of 2022, flooding was recorded in Missouri and Illinois (Greater St. Louis), Eastern Kentucky, Southwest Virginia, parts of West Virginia, the Las Vegas Valley, the Dallas–Fort Worth metroplex, central Mississippi and a flash flood in Zion National Park in Utah. Floods are responsible for deaths, public infrastructure destruction, private property damage and destruction, and public utility loss of facilities and service. All carrying significant costs.

The bottom line is that environmental degradation is costly and destroys wealth. It is caused by the overpopulation of the planet and the inability of this population to incorporate the social costs of its consumption into private costs. When goods and services are underpriced, they are overused and abused, leading to unnecessary depletion of finite resources and the consequences that follow. This overconsumption is generating conditions that increases the temperature of the planet, that fills it and its oceans with garbage from that consumption, that emits harmful elements into the atmosphere affecting people's health and removing the habitat of animals thereby exposing humans to zoonotic diseases. Unfortunately, those contributing most to this degradation are not the ones bearing the major share of the consequential costs and countries with low consumption levels are those with the greatest impacts.

VI (C) – UNSUSTAINABLE DEBT

The *Federal Reserve*, The *US Central Bank*, issued the results of its 2022 survey on Household Economics and reported that 37% of adults, "if faced with an unexpected expense of *US$400*, would either not be able to cover it or would cover it by selling something or borrowing money." In 2013, it was worse as 50% were ill-prepared for such an expense but this has been improving since then with a 4 percentage-points decrease in 2021 from increased savings during the lockdowns and pandemic relief measures enacted in that year. Yet the *US* public debt currently stands at over *US*$32 trillion, or *US*$95,000 per capita, including adults and children. The implication is clear. The *US* public debt, which over the past year has grown by over $2 trillion, is enormous. This is also true for many developed countries.

But it gets worse for the *US*. Its public debt pales in comparison to the total of all other debt including commercial (*US*$12 trillion), household comprising student loans, credit card balances, mortgages, equity loans, and car loans (*US*$16 trillion), and unfunded liabilities such as social security payments, Medicare, Medicaid, and public pensions (estimated at between *US*$122 and *US*$200 trillion in present value terms). Therefore, the *US* per capita total-debt exceeds *US*$0.5 million. And the *US* is not alone. There are other Countries far worse. The table below, **Figure 25**, shows all Countries with public debt exceeding 100% of Country's *GDP* in 2022.

It is understandable why Greece, Lebanon, Italy, and Portugal have had to seek help from the *EU* and *IMF* to stabilize their economies. Excessive debt, in several ways, affects a country's ability to grow. There is

Country's National Debt Exceeding 100% GDP					
Country	*Debt % GDP*	*Country*	*Debt % GDP*	*Country*	*Debt % GDP*
Japan	237	Greece	177	Lebanon	151
Italy	135	Singapore	126	Cape Verde	125
Portugal	117	Angola	111	Bhutan	110
Mozambique	109	United States	107	Djibouti	104
Jamaica	103				

Figure 25

Source: **World Population Review – 2022 Data**

the servicing of the debt that takes money out of the economy and which for Japan with one of the highest debt-to-*GDP* ratios, is about half of the country's tax revenues. As servicing national debt can be costly in terms of raising tax revenues and/or incurring additional debt, governments manipulate the interest rates through their money supply policies to keep these charges at the lowest levels possible. Then there are rating agencies such as Moody's, whose assessments can affect the cost of future debt or its rollover. Again, Japan, overloaded with debt, reduces its sensitivity to rating agencies by having its central bank purchase most of its public debt and the balance held by local banks and trust funds.

Countries with high levels of public debt also tend to have higher than average inflation levels. This is not easily demonstrated as several countries hide inflationary pressures in asset bubbles. But as debt climbs, demand also follows, pushing prices upwards. It is therefore rational to expect that increasing debt, whether spent on capital projects, tax reductions or operational costs, is inflationary as such spending increases demand in the economy without having any impact on the supply side of the equation. But for inflation to appear would put pressure on interest rates thus driving the cost of debt upwards. That is, interest rates would have to be higher than inflation otherwise investors would experience a deterioration in the value of their investments. Central banks of developed countries cannot allow this because debt would become too costly to manage. So, for the last decade or so, since the *Great Financial Recession of 2008*, they have managed to keep interest rates at near zero and even negative. It is this manipulation by the central banks to continue issuing massive amounts of debt that is breaking the relationship between interest rates and inflation. That charade seems to have ended in 2022 as consumer inflation has taken off around the world and the only solution to its reduction is increasing interest rates and all the harm to the servicing of debt that will cause.

One unanticipated consequence of raising interest rates is the impact it has on commercial banks. These banks are allowed to lend a portion of customers' deposits, retaining a smaller portion, referred to as a reserve, to cover withdrawals by the same depositors. Many banks use their reserves to buy Treasury Bills at their low interest rates, because of their perceived liquidity status. But as interest rates rise, the price of these Bills decreases and when sold to cover liquidity needs, the Bank receives proceeds that are lower than their face value. Banks profitability suffers, depositors become anxious and withdraw their deposits not insured by the *Federal Deposit Insurance Corporation*, which current level is *US*$250,000. This "run" on the bank can cause its downfall.

Back to debt-to-*GDP* ratios. So, what is an acceptable ratio trigger-point for a country to be concerned. The *World Population Review (WPR)* is of the opinion this is 77%. It reported that "debt-to-*GDP* ratios above 77% can hinder economic growth and, in some cases, place a country at risk of defaulting on its debts, which could wreak havoc on its economy and financial markets."[17] Although it is not clear what analyses performed by *WPR* support this position, it is still important to understand the quality of the debt incurred. Debt is superior if incurred to build infrastructure and other capital projects rather than fund tax reductions and operational costs. The funding of capital projects adds to a country's development and when their returns exceed the cost of the debt, puts the country on a better footing for economic growth.

Some economists hold the position that the size of a country's debt does not matter if borrowed and repaid in its currency. There may be some validity in that as demonstrated by Japan which national debt is over two times its *GDP* or annual income. It's equivalent to a household consuming over two years of its future income and all the restrictions that would be placed on its future consumption. Others hold that debt only matters if it leads to inflation. These positions are usually used to

---

17 Debt (Public) to *GDP* Ratios by Country, https://worldpopulationreview.com/country-rankings/debt-to-*gdp*-ratio-by-country

support unfunded political programs such as infrastructure spending and social safety-net programs.

The way public debt is funded in the *US*, and other developed countries such as Japan, can be considered of an incestuous nature. The *US* Treasury incurs a deficit by spending more than can be supported by its revenue stream. It then issues bonds (read, *IOUs*) to banks to cover the difference. These Banks in turn sell these bonds to the *US Federal Reserve* which pays for them with *"printed money"*. In effect, the *Federal Reserve*, an arm of Government, churns out printed money to cover the deficit of the Treasury, another arm of the Government. So far, this process has worked because of the high demand for the *US$* from payment of petroleum products (*Petrodollars*) and reserve requirements by foreign countries. But this is fast changing as countries express concern with the *"weaponizing"* of the *US* Dollar by imposing sanctions on countries not conforming to an approved standard of behavior. One such country facing sanctions is Russia for its invasion of Ukraine. Russia, a major supplier of oil and gas, has responded by requiring payment for its energy products, not in dollars but in its currency, rubbles.

In addition, as foreseen by Dr. Eswar S. Prasad in his book, *The Future of Money*[18], digital currencies will transform how we think of money and many countries, including the *US*, have already started studying a new form of currency, *Central Bank Digital Currency*. This will make transfers between countries easier, eliminate the need to pay for imports with a single currency and reduce the dependency on a single currency as a reserve.

The irrefutable fact is that unsustainable debt leads to the debasement of a country's currency requiring more of that currency to pay for imports. This is, by definition, inflationary.

As the problem of the debt pile-up is being postponed to future generations, it raises the question as to how they will deal with it. Very likely, the same way our ancestors, all the way back to Sumerian and

---

18 https://doi.org/10.4159/9780674270091

Babylonian kingships dealt with debt and that is, forgiveness referred to then as debt jubilee, as this usually occurred at celebrated anniversaries. Debt jubilees were a practical way to correct inequalities during celebrations. The concept is well articulated by Dr. Michael Hudson in his book . . . *and forgive them their debts: Lending, Foreclosure and Redemption From Bronze Age To The Jubilee Year[19]*. Debt jubilee has already started in the *US* with a proposal by the Biden administration to forgive a portion of students' loans.

VI (D) – INCOME & WEALTH INEQUALITY

"The income of highest paid in society should never amount to more than five times that of lowest paid."

Plato

Plato, the fourth century *BCE* Greek Philosopher, believed the income of the highest paid in Society should never amount to more than five times that of the lowest paid. But Plato forgot that the highest paid are also the most powerful and in positions to set the rules that realize their greed. In Corporate America, deviations from Plato's formula have been gradual. By 1975, the ratio of *CEOs'* compensation to the mean of employees' pay was 25 to 1. But then escalation took place on a geometric scale. By 1995 it was 112:1 and 2017 312:1. Jeff Bezos, Chairman and former *CEO* of Amazon, purportedly one of the wealthiest individuals on the planet, earns in wealth escalation the annual salary of his $15-per-hour workers every 11.5 seconds. Income and wealth inequality is out of control. The table below (**Figure 26**) show ten countries by their highest

19. . . and forgive them their debts: Lending, Foreclosure and Redemption From Bronze Age Finance to the Jubilee Year. Michael Hudson. ISLET. 2018

Income Gini Index and highest *Wealth Gini Index*, or the worst countries for income and wealth equalities (0 in the *Gini Index* represents the perfect equality where everyone have the same income/wealth, whereas 100 represents the perfect inequality where one person has all the income/wealth and everyone else zero). In reality, the gap between income and wealth inequalities may not be as wide as shown in these tables as many income-inequality measures do not account for taxes and government transfers like healthcare and income support programs. Taxes of a progressive nature would tend to reduce income inequality, make it more equal, so would transfer payments in the form of healthcare, food and housing vouchers, social security, and tax credits.

If a *Wealth Index* of 100 means that all wealth is in the hands of one person, these countries with ranges between 83.7 and 92.6 are symptomatic of the wide concentration in the hands of a few there. Further, it is not accidental that the countries with the worst income/wealth equality,

Highest Net Income Gini Index (%)			Highest Wealth Gini Index (%)		
Country	Income Index	Wealth Index	Country	Wealth Index	Income Index
South Africa	57.7	86.7	Kazakhstan	92.6	28.8
Namibia	55.0	91.0	Egypt	91.7	47.0
Sri Lanka	51.4	66.5	Namibia	91.0	55.0
China	51.0	78.9	Ukraine	90.1	26.3
Zambia	49.5	81.0	South Africa	86.7	57.7
Lesotho	49.3	79.8	United States	85.9	37.8
Columbia	48.9	74.2	Thailand	85.1	43.7
Philippines	47.9	83.9	Lao	84.9	41.1
India	47.9	83.0	Philippines	83.9	47.9
Egypt	47.0	91.7	Indonesia	83.7	45.7

Figure 26

Source: **World Economic Forum, 2018 report**

except the United States, are not among the most advanced/developed. These skewed distributions are not conducive to development.

Income and wealth inequality intensified after the fall of European *Communism* by 1991, and now it's at its highest level. The period of lowest inequality was 1950s to 1980s. So, in the U.S., the top 1% earned 20% of the pretax income in 2013 as opposed to 10% during the period 1950 to 1980. The repercussions are significant for workers' stagnation. Since the *Bolshevik Revolution in 1917* and because of it, Western countries adapted a form of *Capitalism* with a human face. This was referred to as the "*Mixed Economy*". The *Mixed Economy* incorporated the freedoms of a market economy with heavy doses of government intervention in the areas of regulation and transfer payments. Government intervention was intentional and intended to stave off the movement in Western countries towards *Communism* and *Socialism* which had taken hold in Eastern European and Asian countries.

The *Mixed Economy* in Western Countries ended with the fall of *Communism* in Eastern Europe in December 1991. *Capitalism* moved to the forefront. Reagan of the USA and Thatcher of Britain started the dismantling of regulations and transfer payments under the *Mixed Economy* model. They and their cohorts reduced taxes and called for smaller government. They removed tariff barriers so the *Capitalists* could claim a bigger market to sell their goods and services but more importantly to allow the outflow of capital to low-cost labor regions. There was no longer the fear of the attraction of *Communism*, an effective counter-force against the unfairness of *Capitalism*. Workers started falling out of the middle class and income inequalities expanded geometrically.

Additionally, the Governments of the developed countries ramped up their printing presses churning large amounts of paper money. Invariably, this new cash first ended up in the hands of the wealthy through the banking system creating a greater wealth gap.

The problem with widening the income-inequality gap is that it reduces demand for goods and services in the marketplace. Since a greater portion of the pie is going to people whose needs are already being met, and with a lower propensity to consume, the additional income ends up in bank accounts or investment portfolios creating asset inflation. These "bubbles" eventually burst with impacts to the investors but also the remaining 90%. These workers' quality of life continues to stagnate and deteriorate resulting in their anger and the need to find scapegoats.

In a study of *OECD* countries published as a working paper (No. 163) titled *Trends in Income Inequality and its Impact on Economic Growth*, the impacts of growing inequality on per capita *GDP* were modelled. As the independent variable, inequality, affects future *GDP*, the analysis was lagged. For the study, inequality was for the period 1985 to 2005 and the measured impacts were on 1990 to 2010 *GDP* estimates. The analysis shows that the observable data confirms the negative effect income inequality has on economic growth. **Figure 27** reports three outcomes, actual rate of growth, a "counterfactual" rate obtained by subtracting the estimated impact of inequality from actual growth, and impact of inequality rate. The counterfactual rate is therefore the growth rate that would have been observed in the country had inequality not changed (and holding all other variables constant). So, for Mexico, which economy did not grow during the study period, its growth rate would have been around 10% were it not for rising inequality. Several countries, United Kingdom, Finland, Norway, New Zealand, and Mexico are estimated to have reduced growth by around 10 percentage points or more. On the other hand, greater equality helped increase *GDP* per capita in Spain, France, and Ireland.

It adds certainty when the empirical evidence supports theory or logic. It therefore can be concluded that growing income inequality acts as a brake on economic output. Past civilizations have dealt with these inequalities in rash, violent, and ruthless ways and all major revolutions have as its basis the overthrow of those who were benefiting from rent seeking and systems that unfairly distributed the income of a country.

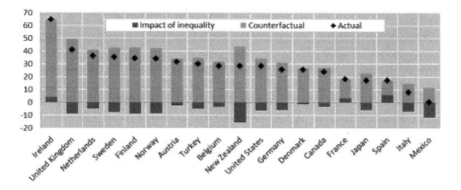

Figure 27

Source: OECD Social, Employment and Migration Working Paper 163

That was the case with the French, Russian and Chinese revolutions which all had the notion of égalité foremost in their upheaval of the existing order.

And current trends of social unrest with both income and wealth inequalities will be no different. The pushback to inequalities started in 2011 with *Occupy Wall Street*, a protest in Zuccotti Park, New York City, against economic inequality. It continues in more recent times with protests in France with the *Gilets Jaunes* (yellow vests) movement. Who would imagine Paris burning, again, by protesters seeking economic justice? And these riots will only escalate.

VI (E) – DESPAIRING ELECTORATE

"Free market competition can do many things, but there are also many areas where it cannot work well, including in the provision of healthcare, the exorbitant cost of which is doing immense harm to the health and wellbeing of America."

Anne Case & Angus Deaton

This section draws on research done by economists Anne Case and Angus Deaton and published in their book, *Death of Despair: and The Future of Capitalism*[20]. The research clearly demonstrates that white, blue-collar workers without the benefit of a tertiary education, are in despair and increasingly turning to accidental poisonings (mainly drug overdoses), suicides, and alcoholic addiction, the latter inducing diseases to the liver and heart. Added to mortalities are morbidities where workers dissatisfied and deluded with their way-of-life are neglecting their health needs, and obesity, diabetes and other diseases are on the rise. They are also supporting nativistic and anti-immigration ideas associated with the discredited political economy of fascism and have shown or expressed the intention of implementing these ideas through violent change.

Americans most affected by globalization and technology are middle-aged and white. Many in this subset have gone from middle-class status working in manufacturing or in coal mining jobs, not requiring more than a high-school education, to lower paying service jobs or outsourced low-skill jobs affecting their prospects for marriage, raising a family, taking a vacation, and owning a home, all associated with middle-class living. **Figure 28** shows the effect of this trend on Kentuckians where a small deviation between tertiary educated and their less-educated middle-aged white counterparts in the early 1990s, took off at the turn of the century to a significant gap fifteen years later. Kentucky is the third largest state for coal mining behind West Virginia and Pennsylvania.

The way non-college, middle-aged labor can recover from its displacement is by increasing productivity, as its displacement is caused by this labor being over-priced. The larger the doses of capital added to labor in the manufacturing process, as attested by the technological advances, the higher its productivity. Unfortunately, labor is so over-priced in the *US* and uncompetitive, that although the economy is growing, it

---

20   Case, Anne, and Angus Deaton. 2020. Deaths of Despair and the Future of Capitalism. Princeton, NJ: Princeton University Press.

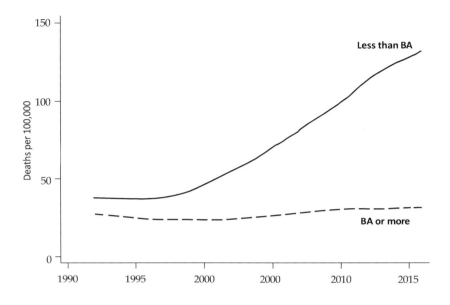

Figure 28 Suicide, drug overdose, and alcoholic liver disease mortality in Kentucky, by educational attainment, white non-Hispanics ages 45–54. Case/Deaton calculations using Centers for Disease Control and Prevention data.

is not translating into increases in wages. Case/Deaton reported that between 1979 to 2017, the average growth in median wages of white men without a bachelor's degree was minus 0.2 percent per year. Despite their improved productivity, their wages were still being driven down by the market.

Although this chapter will concentrate on white despair as this demography was affected most by loss of middle-class status since the 1990s, middle-aged blacks have higher general mortality rates than their white counterparts. Parallels to the conditions of middle-aged whites with less than a college education were experienced by Blacks in the 1970s with the loss of blue-collar manufacturing jobs in the Northern cities as firms shifted from these jobs to service ones. In addition, in the 1980s, their communities were in crisis from crack-cocaine, a relatively inexpensive street drug, and *HIV*. But Black mortality rates have been falling since the year 2000 whereas White rates have been rising. This has narrowed the gap since 2000 by about half from about 400 deaths per 100,000 people to below 200 deaths by 2017. That's not the case with mortality from suicides/drug overdoses/alcoholism. Starting in the early 2000s, white middle-aged rates have exceeded that of blacks within both subsets, those with and without a college degree. And although these rates are increasing among both blacks and whites, they have been expanding between them.

Figure 29, developed by Case and Deaton, shows this trend. By 2000, Black midlife workers with less than a tertiary education were on par with White compatriots. But although by 2017 their rates were both on an upward trajectory, the gap from mortality due to alcohol and suicides, had increased significantly among the White population.

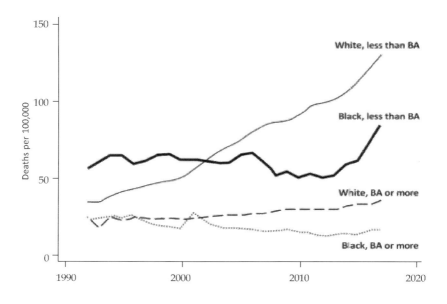

Figure 29 **Drug, alcohol, and suicide mortality in midlife, 1992–2017, blacks and whites, with and without a college degree. Case/Deaton calculations using Centers for Disease Control and Prevention data, ages 45–54 (age adjusted).**

Interestingly, this is not the case with White workers in other developed countries, such as France, United Kingdom, and Sweden. Although mortality rates for middle-aged Whites in France were higher than that of their comparison groups in the US in 1990, that changed in the early 2000s and the trend is for the US mortality rates to continue increasing whereas that of France, UK and Sweden are declining.

Further as Case and Deaton convincingly argue, the wasteful cost of healthcare in the US is a major contributor to the despair of Americans, especially the working class. It is not only the over-prescription of opioids and provision of poor treatment, but the transformation of healthcare in the US from a societal right to a profit center operated by private equity firms. Hospitals, at their inception, were institutions for the poor and low-income citizens as the rich had their private doctors take care of their medical needs in the comfort of their homes. This process has changed, and hospitals are now managed by well-paid CEOs whose compensation is directly linked to the profitability of the institutions, thereby transferring income and wealth from the poor to the wealthy. Ridiculous examples of this are given with shared rooms costing US$10,000 daily with everything else extra including television.

An investigation was done by the New York Times and reported on September 24, 2022, under the title *Profits Over Patients: They Were Entitled to Free Care. Hospitals Hounded Them to Pay*, found that more than half the US hospitals are nonprofits enjoying lucrative tax exemptions, but many of them have become indistinguishable from for-profit hospitals focusing on their bottom-line. One such hospital included in the investigation is Providence, founded by Nuns in the 1850s but which now owns 51 hospitals and more than 900 clinics producing revenues exceeding $27 billion. Providence, as a nonprofit, avoids more than $1 billion per year in taxes, but has adopted measures to extract the maximum income from patients even those who are exempted from charges or are entitled to discounted rates. Nonprofits have used aggressive measures to go after revenues from low-income patients such as debt collectors, garnished wages, and reporting payment-delinquencies to credit agencies. The *CEOs* of these nonprofits are handsomely compensated for their bottom-line results, and in the case of Providence, its *CEO*, Dr. Hochman, earned $10 million in 2020.

So, the health care industry, from its market power due to the size of its members, is a major contributor to *Deaths of Despair*. It accomplishes this with high medical fees, exacerbating income inequality through transfers from poor to wealthy, and exercising influence on the political class protecting their self-interests and those of their backers. For the nonprofits, they have found ways to fund their rent-seeking activities while receiving financial support from taxpayers. The good news is even service industries with high profit margins and costs, attract technological changes which are designed to reduce these exploitations, and already robotics and offshoring are slowly being incorporated in the industry. These are the same trends that affected manufacturing jobs at the turn of the Century, as wages became over-priced in that industry.

Further, health care is a service not properly allocated by the market as choices are compromised by patients under duress or in physical and mental states not conducive to rational decision-making. And because patients in many cases are not aware of the costs being incurred, as in these cases, costs are borne by Companies through their insurance coverage, and governments, their demand for healthcare is not a function of price. Their co-pay may have some mitigating effects but not the effect knowing the full cost would have had. But workers' compensation is negatively affected because of the benefit companies provide their employees and which cannot pay more due to the already high cost of labor. Wages in real terms shrink and workers fall behind, unable to provide a lifestyle previously enjoyed or part of their lives growing up. The high cost of healthcare is a major contributor to the despair filtering through blue-collar workers in the *US*.

But costs, with associated inefficiencies, are not expected to abate anytime soon because of the significant lobbying investment by the healthcare industry. In 2018, the lobbyists in this industry were 5 times the number of members of Congress, many coming from the ranks of ex-Congress members or ex-staffers. The industry spent *US*$567 million on lobbying and *US*$133 million on support to actual or potential members. As seen before, politicians are keen to do the bidding of their lobbying supporters even to the detriment of the constituents. Solutions to this inefficient healthcare system, especially when compared to other developed countries in delivering results, will be difficult to reverse with all the special interests, opposed to delivering efficient results, built in.

The progression to a despairing population was 50 years in the making, having had its origins with the reintroduction of fiat currency in the *US* in the 1970s. Before then, middle-class lifestyles were characterized by single-earner families. Men participation in the workforce was around 80%. But cost-of-living increases started taking a toll and by the 1970s, women family members were forced to take paid jobs to make ends meet. This era was characterized by latch-key kids who, as no parent was home to greet them from school, had to let themselves into their homes. According to *BLS* data, women participation in the workforce increased by 14 percentage points (from 46.3% to 60.1%) over the 25 years starting in the mid-1970s. Further deterioration took place as households reduced savings and increased debt to meet living costs. A *Federal Reserve* survey in 2013 found that 50% of households didn't have $400 in savings, and debt incurred by them rose $5.1 trillion between 2013 ($11.15 trillion) and 2022 ($16.16 trillion). Further, about 70% live paycheck to paycheck, a clear outcome from servicing large debts. The evolution to deterioration is obvious with Moms forced into the workforce, families exhausting their savings, families incurred large amounts of debt, and now the ultimate stage – increasing homelessness estimated at around 600,000 in 2022. Despair indeed!

PART 2

SOLUTIONS

VII

CHANGING COURSE

No, the sky is not falling, but instead, it's a case of the emperor having no clothes. And no one seems to have the fortitude to tell the emperor that the decline in the wellbeing of Americans is rooted in the introduction of fiat currency in the early 1970s, allowing for the unconstrained "printing" of money, the very definition of inflation. Allowing for racking up large public debt which stands at around $95,000 per capita and cannot be repaid. Forgiving debt has already started with a government's proposal to forgive some students' loans. And allowing for an increasing portion of the country's *GDP* going to fewer people, the essence of violent historical revolutions is in the making.

One attribute of money is a store of value. This means that money is essentially an asset that maintains its future value and can be exchanged then without much or any deterioration. So how could fiat money, without any intrinsic value, as it cost the same to print or create a $1 note as a $100 note, have value beyond the estimated $0.05 printing cost? Because the emperor says that $100 note has 100 times the value of a $1 note, shouldn't make it so. What's next—"*you will own nothing and be happy*"! Well, that's not as outlandish, but who knows, you may well be happy. But the emperor needs to be made aware of his nakedness.

121

Another clear case of the clothes-less emperor is population control. Over the past 50 years, the world population has more than doubled leading to consumption levels and patterns damaging to its environment. According to our scientists, the environmental degradation will cause much misery and hardships, floodings and droughts, famine, and pestilence, but instead of addressing the existential issue of over-population, the forces that be are tackling symptoms of this over population. They are searching for measures to limit our carbon footprint—carbon capture, substituting non-carbon producing energy technologies for fossil fuel use, and preserving forests and peat lands that already store vast amounts of greenhouse gases. China, until recently, was the only country to have implemented a successful population control structure with its one-child-per-family program. But it has since been abandoned as it was for the wrong reasons—to free its existing population from the burden of child rearing and improve its chances of climbing out of poverty. It worked and improved the lot of many Chinese families, but as soon as forecast indicated a shortage of labor, China mitigated its population reduction program.[21]

And the emperor has no clothes with respect to governments' monetary management of the economy not in dissimilar ways some command economies managed their economies by ignoring the markets and deter-mining what and how much to produce. Ignoring market forces in the production of goods often led to their shortages and surpluses resulting in the misapplication of resources. Managing a country's monetary system by setting inflation and employment targets, influencing GDP levels funded by debt, setting interest rates and the money supply, lead

---

21 Unless managed properly, population control programs can have serious demographic con-sequences. During the period the population restrictions was in place, Chinese families, favoring male over female children, created a skewed population distribution with a severe shortage of females. Women, as they attain higher levels of education, are more selective of their partners, preferring men with higher qualifications and potential incomes. The less qualified men were found less attractive and had to seek partners in other Asian countries.

to asset inflation/bubbles through corporate stock buybacks, speculative stock market interventions, increased demand for real estate especially during *Quantitative Easing*, again distorting the allocations of the markets and thus the introduction of inefficiencies in the economy. The *US* is not immune from such inefficiencies as it continues to rack up deficits and debts. It has however delayed the harsh consequences of hyperinflation by having the Dollar designated as a reserve currency, having other nations accept dollars in settlement of payments and debts, and the payment for oil and gas be conducted in dollars (*Petrodollars*). The impulse by the *US* and developed countries to print their way out of difficult decision making seems to have a terminal timeframe.

VII (A) – TETHERED CURRENCY

Our current monetary system is plagued with problems of requiring loyalty for its survival (fiat currency), of slough and cost in its execution (forex transactions), of un-traceability in its distribution (cash), of speculative disastrous outcomes to its institutions (bank runs), and of monopolization with its utilization (imposition of sanctions). With so many serious problems, leaving all untouched and for over half a century, the end of the road is in sight. It's time for a reset, one that backs currencies with assets, can be zipped around the world at little costs and at the speed of bandwidth, one where currency is traceable thereby greatly reducing incidence of crime, one that eliminates the reliance of commercial banks in brokering customer deposits, and one that cannot be used in the enforcement of sanctions. The system proposed in this book would address all those problems, and consists of three subsets, a World Central Bank, countries' central banks, and commercial banks.

The most serious of the problems is that of fiat currency. It leads to value inconsistency arising from countries that try to print their way out of a failing economy usually to fund debt. As their currencies are not tied to anything of value, it's an easy decision to implement. So, the greatest value the reset can provide is giving currency intrinsic value, such as gold and other assets. Gold has had value even before the ancient Mesopotamian societies of Sumer, Akkad, Assyria, and Babylon mainly as high-status regalia and for religious purposes before evolving to the status of a medium of exchange. It was selected and used as the first money when ancient societies needed to move away from a transfer system of bartering.

But gold is heavy and costly to transport around. A tried solution, paper currency not backed by precious metals or commodities, or fiat currency, was imposed on the Chinese people of the Yuan dynasty by Kublai Khan in the 13th century. This was so revolutionary and senseless to the Chinese then, that acceptance of the decree could only take place on "pain of death". Fiat currency was recently resurrected and is currently the universal nature of money, not through threats of death, but by the emperors being clueless to the damage it causes. Damage such as the hyperinflation that caused 13th century China to abandon fiat currency after over-printing to fund its wars. Wars seem to be the catalyst that causes major shifts in monetary systems as it was the funding of the Vietnam war that led the Americans to abandon the gold standard of the 1944 *Bretton Woods Agreement*. And undoubtedly, the Ukrainian war in Europe is a major mechanism for the realignment of nations behind optional payment systems such as *BRICS*, emerging on the world market. This may solve some of the problems associated with the current monetary structure, but the majority still burdens the system.

With respect to the slough and cost of the system, the World Bank estimates that sending remittances to low- and middle-income countries is about 7% of the transfer value. And these transfers can take days to reach their destinations. This is due to the number of intermediary banks the money must be cleared through, all members of the messaging network, *Society for Worldwide Interbank Financial Telecommunications (SWIFT)*, and each implementing charges for its participation in the transaction.

VII (A) 1 – FINANCIAL RESET, OUTLINE

The fix to all monetary problems is the elimination of fiat currencies and replacing them with a universal currency backed by assets found in all countries with value on the world market. This is accomplished with the introduction of a universal digital currency (*WBDC*) managed by a *World Central Bank (WCB)*, the central bank of all central banks. In this scenario, the *WCB* would identify assets, used to back its *WBDC*, under three broad categories, minerals/metals, arable lands, and carbon sinks[22]. Minerals and metals would consist of many components including gold, silver, copper, bauxite/alumina, rare-earth, oil and gas, uranium etc. Arable lands could be divided by tropical, temperate, and polar zones to recognize that such lands in one zone could have a different productivity/value than that in another zone. And carbon sinks cover areas of forests, peat lands, and permafrost of the Artic land surface capturing huge amounts of methane greenhouse gasses.

Having identified the assets that will be used to back its *WBDC*, the process would then develop the capacity of each country to produce these assets and the quantities they can produce. By then applying a world market price, stated in *WBDC* units[23], to each asset by country, a total *WBDC* can be constructed along with each country's contribution to the total. For example, **Figure 30** shows a simplified outcome of this analysis using two countries, *A & B*, and six currency assets.

---

22 This is the author's opinion, but the list of assets could be whatever is agreeable to by most countries. What's important here is the concept, not the details.

23 How to determine the value of a new currency? There are several approaches, but the one favored by the Author is one using an algorithm tied to the value of gold. This requires setting the currency at the price of an ounce of gold which currently is about *US*$2,000 per ounce. So, one *WBDC* can purchase one ounce of gold and all other assets, such as a barrel of oil and gas, would be valued in terms of an ounce of gold, or about 0.04 *WBDC* (80/2,000). Fraction of currencies is facilitated by the use of digital currencies. Eventually, demand and supply forces will refine these price relationships.

Simplified Computation of World Bank Digital Currency – 2 Countries						
A *Currency Assets*	**B** *Country A Quantity*	**C** *Country B Quantity*	**D** *Market Value (WBDC)*	**E** *Country A (WBDC 000)* *B x D*	**F** *Country B (WBDC 000)* *C x D*	**G** *Total (WBDC 000)* *E + F*
Gold – ounces	5,000	25,000	2,000	10,000	50,000	60,000
Oil & Gas – Barrels	100,000	50,000	100	10,000	5,000	15,000
Uranium – tons	0	40	1,000	0	40	40
Rare Earth – kg	2,500	3,000	550	1,375	1,650	3,025
Arable Land – acres	20,000	25,000	3,000	60,000	75,000	135,000
Forests – Carbon credit/acre	55,000	75,000	50	2,750	3,750	6,500
Total				**84,125**	**135,440**	**219,565**

Figure 30

The World Central Bank would, from this analysis, deposit WBDC84.125 million in the reserve account of Country A and WBDC135.44 million in that of Country B. A country can only change its reserves by discovering new resources identified by the WCB as appropriate in backing currencies, having its quantities and market value of these assets change, and/or by cross-border transactions. A country cannot increase its reserves, nor can the WCB, by "printing" WBDCs. The total amount of WBDCs, shown in the above example at WBDC219.565 million, is constrained by the availability of currency assets and their market values. The movement of *WBDCs* among countries is done by the *WCB* in real time by adjusting their reserves. By eliminating all the corresponding and intermediary banks of the current system and replacing them with one bank, the *WCB*, transactions are sped up, record-keeping simplified, and costs reduced. And there is no role for speculators to play in determining the exchange rate among currencies as all countries would use the same currency in cross-border transactions. An added benefit, as it remains a centralized ledger, it eliminates the need for the draconian measures imposed on the banking systems of developing countries by the developed countries to control the flow of funds they fear may be for the purpose of funding terrorist activities or laundering money.

A *WBDC* would solve the problems associated with cross-border payments. But *WBDCs* may also be used for domestic functions, such as payments for goods and services, settling debts and paying taxes. Countries adopting the *WBDC* as their official currencies would require their central banks to determine their currencies' conversion rates. But when the conversion is completed, that country's currency will be on par with the world currency, the *WBDC*. However, no country is forced to convert to the *WBDC* as countries can maintain a national currency such as the dollar or pound for domestic transactions despite these being fiat currencies. But all cross-border transactions would have to be settled in *WBDCs*, no national currencies in this arena.

WBDCs are not fixed and can be increased by changes in country quantities and the market price of country assets included in each country's asset register at the *WCB* to support growth. For example, if we consider the periodic update to each country's asset register for changes in quantities of assets and their prices, using the simplified model in **Figure 31**, and assuming the price of oil doubled to *WBDC*200 per barrel and country *A* discovered more gold raising its level to 35,000 ounces from 5,000. These two changes would increase country *A*'s *WBDC* from *WBDC*10 million to *WBDC*70 million, and the increase in the price of oil, increases both countries' *WBDCs* by 15 million.

Simplified Computation of World Digital Currency Update - 2 Countries						
A	B	C	D	E	F	G
Currency Assets	Country A Quantity	Country B Quantity	Market Value (WBDC)	Country A (WBDC 000) $B \times D$	Country B (WBDC 000) $C \times D$	Total (WBDC 000) $E + F$
Gold – ounces	35,000	25,000	2,000	70,000	50,000	120,000
Oil & Gas – Barrels	100,000	50,000	200	20,000	10,000	30,000
Uranium – tons	0	40	1,000	0	40	40
Rare Earth – kg	2,500	3,000	550	1,375	1,650	3,025
Arable Land – acres	20,000	25,000	3,000	60,000	75,000	135,000
Forests – Carbon credit/acre	55,000	75,000	50	2,750	3,750	6,500
Total				154,125	140,440	294,565

Figure 31

As these two countries represent the world economy in the hypothetical example, the world currency value would increase by about 34%. It is this periodic updating that allows for the expansion/contraction of the world's money supply instead of the current arbitrary approach to meet some political goal.

As *WBDCs* are assets as well as claims on assets and can be exchanged for those of any country, the probability is low that a country would exhaust all its assets. In an extreme case, a country could have no physical assets in its ledger of the *WCB* but could have *WBDCs*, a true store of value.

VII (A) 2 – FINANCIAL RESET, PLAYERS

Another major benefit is the changing roles of commercial banks by the reset. Currently, their key function is brokering short-term deposits to long-term loans, referred to as maturity transformation. This is characterized by low interest payments by commercial banks to depositors for their deposits (costs) and receipts of higher interest rates (income) from longer-term borrowers. The funding of long-term projects has the beneficial effect of increasing the economy's output and employment. The problem occurs when depositors panic and rush for the exit or withdraw their deposit for higher yielding investments, commercial banks are put under pressure and extraordinary measures are needed to maintain liquidity and avoid their collapse. Bank runs, which can be destructive to the economy's finance sector, are only possible because commercial banks are allowed to receive deposits from which they earn their incomes, and they are numerous such banks. Bank runs cannot exist in the absence of deposits, and with a single depositary. Thus, the elimination of bank runs is accomplished by removing the role of commercial banks as depositaries of currency and requiring that they be capitalized similar to other business ventures, with equity and debt, and not by deposits.

Under this new approach, runs on commercial banks, which invariably lead to failure affecting their continued viability, will be a phenomenon of the past. There would be no need for deposits to be held at commercial banks as all deposits would be held at central banks where they were initially issued. Commercial banks would continue to provide loans, not as a fractional portion of deposits, but from shareholders' equity and debt. The source of these loans can be both investors and central banks, the latter leveraging customer deposits to provide loans, and the resulting income used to fund operations.

So, commercial banks would continue their important role of maturity transformation, where banks bundle loans with different term durations, into long-term funding for projects that benefit the economy. They would need less staff to process cash and check transactions as all would be electronically conducted, and thus would be much more efficient in their operations.

The role of Central Banks will also change. This would be limited to maintaining accounts for all depositors and settling their transactions, all in digital currencies; make loans to commercial banks; in the event a country decides to maintain a separate national currency, determine the exchange rate with the *WBDC*; and settle offshore transactions in its ledger with the *WCB*. In this new role, central banks will speed up transactions, reduce, if not eliminate, money-type crime, eliminate bank runs, and reduce the cost and time of offshore transactions.

The new *WCB* role is the estimation of each country's *WBDC*, maintain a register of these estimates, and settle all cross-border transactions. This removes the reckless printing of currency from that of the Central Bank, gives a basis for expanding the money supply (expansion of *WBDCs*), and puts a check on hyperinflation.

VII (A) 3 – FINANCIAL RESET, SUMMARY

In summary, the solution to what ails the world today from the use of fiat currency, money that is expected to be a store of value but without intrinsic value, is a universal currency managed by an organization such as a *World Central Bank*. This currency would be backed by assets with value on a worldwide basis including metals and minerals used in the manufacture of commodities, carbon credits representing contributions from a country's carbon sinks used to internalize environmental costs, and arable land used in feeding the world population. As the construction of this asset class will impact countries which will try to have their assets included in the asset class as it impacts the amount on *WBDCs* they receive, the criterion should ultimately be whether the asset has universal application and thus widespread demand. A desert country may have tons of sand but unless there is a wide demand for sand from the world population, sand may not be an asset included in the currency asset class. Universal demand is an important condition to satisfy because for an asset to have value, it must have widespread demand, be capable of transferability, and capable of changing ownership. So, assets backing a universal currency should meet these criteria. This is not to suggest that transferability would be without restrictions. First, the transferability of fungible assets such as minerals and metals should be on a bullion-size basis, say a minimum of 1 billion *WBDCs*, to avoid the multitude of cashing-ins that could otherwise take place. Second, only fungible assets would qualify for transfer among countries. Non-fungible, such as farmlands would be off the table for country transfers, as some countries would not want other countries to own their land, so such transfers should not be automatic. All transfers among countries would be recorded and kept track of by the *WCB*, and within countries, by their central banks.

In the reset, the role of central banks is to ensure there are workable mechanisms to generate adequate liquidity to support growth in their economies, provide settlement services for all depositors, maintain deposit accounts for all customers (this is no longer a function of the commercial banks), and manage their balances at the *WCB*.

And for those central banks adopting the *WBDC* as their national currency, they would also be responsible for the initial exchange of their fiat currencies for *WBDCs*, including the determination of the exchange rate. So, if a country decides to treat its currency on par with the *WBDC*, all deposits held by its central bank would be replaced with *WBDCs* on a one-to-one basis. Some allowance would have to be made for the exchange of fiat currency held by small, low-income individuals, who for some reason or other, did not or could not open deposit accounts at commercial banks. But generally, currency outside the banking system should not be allowed to participate in the exchange process because of the high probability that it was illegally obtained.

The *WCB* determines the money supply of each country by identifying the list of currency assets, the stock of these assets held by each country, and the value of each asset. The *WCB* also maintains a centralized ledger of the assets of all countries as it performs the essential function of providing settlement services between countries. Under this dispensation, the *WCB* will be self-supporting by charging a small fee for services it provides such as Settlements among Central Banks. It will also offer loans to Member Nations earning income from interest spreads between lending and borrowing Nations. Central Banks can also follow this model for services they provide their commercial banks.

VII (B) – DEFLATIONARY POLICIES & TRANSITORY INCOME SUPPORT

The *US*, like many other developed countries, has a major problem partly caused by inflation targeting, but also from anti-market measures, political in nature, such as minimum-wage legislation and the legalization of labor cartels. Consequently, as its cost of living has risen, so has the cost of labor to the level that it is overpriced and no longer competitive. A commodity is overpriced when it can readily be replaced by cheaper alternatives such as, in the case of labor, technology and/or outsourcing/offshoring to lower-priced regions and countries. American workers don't add enough value to commodities produced, or to their numbers (known as labor productivity), to justify the difference in their compensation. American workers in the manufacturing sector earn six time more than workers in Mexico, nine times more than China and a whooping 24 times more than Indian workers. As with all products that are overpriced, their demand declines until they become expendable.

Yet, even at these high levels of compensation, workers are finding it difficult to keep abreast of the cost of living, especially housing and food.

A study by the Comprehensive Income Dataset Project at UChicago found that about 40% of unhoused individuals in the U.S. had earnings from formal employment, and more than half of the sheltered homeless adult population under age 65 worked at some point. And it's estimated that there are half a million homeless individuals in the *US*.

Gig work is on the rise with workers having to hold down multiple jobs to make ends meet, and the jobs available are in government and the service sectors like warehousing and hospitality. Service sector jobs cannot be offshored but are vulnerable to displacement by technology as witnessed by the robots easily and safely moving around an Amazon warehouse. For those service jobs requiring the transportation of persons or delivery of goods, autonomous vehicles, delivery drones, and other robotic devices are on the horizon.

The pandemic took out so many workers either through mortality, morbidity, and retirement, and pumped so much funding support into the *US* economy, that the result was a temporary reprieve for labor and its compensation. Unemployment rates declined and wage growth increased. This emboldened labor in pushing to have its unions recognized at facilities of some major employers such as Amazon and Starbucks. A miscalculation from a misunderstanding of the causes of the demand for labor, and which reaction of promoting labor unions and wage hikes, will only hasten labor's demise.

And the politicians had to get involved with measures that produce more consequential harm than good. The Biden's administration is reported to propose rule changes that could make it easier for millions of truckers, Uber drivers, freelance writers, home care workers, and janitors to be classified as employees rather than independent contractors—a shift that would grant them access to a host of federal labor protections, such as minimum wages, overtime, unemployment insurance and social security benefits. Fortunately, surveys show most gig workers prefer their gig status as seen in a 2018 report by the *Bureau of Labor Statistics* which stated that 79% of independent contractors preferred their contracting arrangement over a traditional job. Further, such reclassifications have not made it past the federal appeals courts. That's fortunate as such a rule would have strengthened the provisions of the 1938 Fair Labor Standards Act, one of the Acts that has led to the conundrum the relevance of labor is now facing.

The American worker, sensing a lack of relevance in the emerging world order, is anxious and despairing. As outlined in sub-Chapter VI (e), job losses in the manufacturing and mining sectors are causing social disruptions, suicides by drug overdoses, increased support for authoritarian and fascist rule, and nativistic sentiments. This is clearly the case in the *US* with the January 6, 2021 attack on the Capitol, support for Donald Trump and his Republican party, illiberal positions on trade, and migrant bashing. And these positions aren't limited to the *US*. In Europe, Italy and Sweden have elected representatives who are expected to promulgate and put into practice many of these positions, and the trend could extend to Spain, France, and Germany in the future. The *UK* has already exited the European Union to have more control of its borders. These developed countries have brought the problem on themselves by believing they could inflate their economies without consequences of offsetting increased productivity. That didn't work out and now is the time to reverse policy.

But in addition to inflationary increases to the cost of living, its level has also been impacted by legislation implemented way back in the 1930s — *The National Labor Relations Act (NLRA)* of 1935 and the *Fair Labor Standards Act (FLSA)* of 1938, and their amendments. Both Acts, *NLRA* guarantees the right of private sector employees to organize into unions, bargain with employers and engage in strikes, and the *FLSA* sets minimum wages and overtime pay, would increase labor costs over and above those determined by a free market. By 2009, the minimum wage had risen to $7.25/hour from $0.40 when the Act was passed in 1938. The minimum wage has not changed since 2009, a clear recognition that labor is already over-priced, but, very few workers, if any, accept this low minimum wage given the cost-of-living levels they are faced with. They simply could not survive on such an income but States as well as unofficial minimum wages have more than double the official one. The only way to bring a country's cost of living down is to deflate the economy, that is reduce the demand for goods, services, and investments to cause the price levels to decrease. And because labor legislation, specifically the *NLRA* and *FLSA*, along with their amendments are partly responsible, they should be repealed. As the *US* labor uncompetitiveness is due largely to its high cost of living, this deflation will cause much hardship to the population. Indeed, bitter medicine.

Deflating an economy is accomplished by reducing broad demand for goods and services to induce a recession, defined as negative growth in *GDP* for at least two consecutive quarters. The preferred way to a recession is to allow market forces to take control of the economy and especially with the *US* government sector carrying over $32 trillion in public debt. This is an enormous sum exceeding *GDP* and will have consequences. The market will increase the interest rate acknowledging the risk of repayment of such a large sum of money. As the cost of debt increases, demand which was funded by debt will start to decrease, not only in the government sectors but all sectors of the economy. The *US* economy may be slightly more resilient due to its currency, the dollar, being used by other countries as a reserve currency for paying for imports and debt, but there should be no doubt that if left unfettered, the market would cause interest rates to rise given the amount of debt in the *US* economy.

But although the market is an efficient allocator of resources and capable of correcting for the misapplication of these resources, it does not always accomplish this in a manner Humans consider to be fair and equitable. The market is more suited for the jungle, survival of the fittest, which social compact humans have long rejected. Market solutions, which violate its sense of fairness and equity, should therefore be modified to remove its harsh aspects. And the solution of inducing a recession and even a depression to bring the *US* and other developed countries' cost-of-living and consequently wage rates down, is a harsh one with much anguish and pain to those who would be affected. This is therefore a case where the effects from corrective action need to be mitigated.

The unemployment rate rises during recessions and depressions. There are some safety nets in developed countries, such as unemployment insurance, but they are temporary measures not meant for corrections that will probably take several years. An income support program is needed for workers whose income has fallen below the cost of living either because they are now unemployed, or the market has assessed their contributions below wages previously obtained.

The income support for these workers should not return them to what pertained before deflationary measures were implemented and caused their retrenchment or reduction in earnings, as this would defeat the exercise of lowering the cost of living. It is recommended that this support provide for their minimum needs of food, shelter, transportation, and utilities, and where children are involved, income support to allow the continuation of their education along with minimum needs. This support would be targeted not unlike food and housing vouchers and best implemented after currencies have been digitized as discussed in the previous sub-chapter, VII (a). A *centralized digital currency* system has several advantages over the current one in that it greatly reduces if not eliminates cash-related crimes such as theft, money laundering, tax avoidance, and aid to terrorist organizations, but also as it is digital, transfers can be made in real time and expenditures targeted to specific organizations or individuals. For example, transfers for housing deposited in an individual account can only be paid into a landlord's bank account, and that of food to a grocery store/supermarket. These accounts also allow for verification of earnings on a real-time basis to determine eligibility for income support. These income support programs would not require a large government bureaucracy to manage and can be done automatically after qualification criteria and levels of support have been established.

In summary, as it was inflation, intentional or unintentional introduced in the economy, along with anti-market labor legislations which is causing labor to be expendable in the economies of the *US* and developed countries, the solution is a reversal of the process by deflating the economy and rescinding the harmful labor laws. But because of the length of time the problem was allowed to percolate, the damage is widespread. Labor is no longer competitive and except for government and service sectors where mobility is restricted, have been offshored or displaced by technology. And the replacement process is ongoing with awesome technologies on the horizon.

Labor, sensing its irrelevance, is despairing, and engaging in behaviors that are self-harming, and adopting illiberal positions such as nativism, encouraged by the political classes to distract from the real causes of short-termism and self-interests in politics. In the *US*, these positions are encapsulated in political slogans such as *"Make America Great Again"*, *"America First"* and *"Made in America"*. But slogans aren't solutions. For example, *"Made in America"* is a slogan of the Biden administration meant to bring back offshoring jobs to America with the help of sizable subsidies as in the *CHIPS and Science Act of 2022*, which will invest $250 billion in research and development, over the next five years, to help the U.S. regain a leading position in semiconductor chip manufacturing industry. The Biden administration is also focused on Buy American Act of 1933, which requires federal funds to be spent on locally produced goods, by increasing the local content in the definition of American made goods and services. The Trump administration imposed increased tariff on Chinese imports and renegotiated the trade agreement with Canada and Mexico, *North American Free Trade Agreement (NAFTA)*, as solutions to the decline of labor. As the root cause of the problem, the country's high cost of living, was not addressed by either the Trump or the Biden administrations in their proposals, these measures will not provide meaningful solutions, but instead are intended to distract workers from the true interests of politicians with these superficial solutions. The practice of central banks intervening in the market to change interest rates and the money supply, despite the evidence that such interventions result in asset inflation and not that of consumer inflation, which is more reactive to fiscal measure, should also cease as the market has solutions to problems that arise in the economy. There is no need for central banks' intervention to this extent in the economy and it's akin to the failed model of the planned economy of Eastern Europe before the late 1980s.

VII (C) – RESTRICTIONS ON DEBT

Debt, without the prospects of generating a return equivalent to or higher than its amortization, will threaten future growth in an economy. Despite this, the political elite has promoted debt as a tool to increase short-term *GDP*, an index of wellbeing. These politicians have therefore self-benefited from both public and private debt. Thus, as public debt grows, future generations are saddled with its repayment.

Currently, there are thirteen countries which public debt exceeds their annual *GDP*, including the USA, with another seven countries in the ninety-percentage range. The major debtor is Japan with debt more than two years of its *GDP*. This is analogous to a household incurring debt greater than twice its annual earnings, an untenable situation, as some countries in this unenvied group have found out. Greece, Lebanon, Italy and Portugal, countries with public debts higher than their annual *GDP*, have all had financial problems, including potential defaults, requiring the intervention of the *EU* or *IMF*. Japan is forced to keep interest rates low to be able to service its debt and accomplishes this through having a large portion of its debt, 43%, held by the Bank of Japan. But low interest rates in the face of global commodity price hikes and contrary to remedial actions in other countries, have resulted in the yen falling to a 24-year low, putting further pressure on domestic prices. Remarkably however, Japan's consumer inflation rate, as reported by the World Economic Forum, stands at 3% at July 2022, low in comparison to other *G7* countries. Apparently, this relatively low rate is due to certain State price-controls, and an ageing population tempering demand.

Investors are starting to understand that countries cannot continue to print their way to prosperity. In a World Bank study, countries that maintained a debt-to-*GDP* ratio of over 77% for prolonged periods of time experienced economic slowdowns. These investors are starting to exercise more caution and less recklessness in participating in these capital markets. A recent *UK* financial crisis, to be elaborated further in this chapter, is a case in point.

And why do some countries with high debt levels fare better than others? The evidence is that some of those that seem to have avoided a financial crisis from their debt levels, are countries with assets similar to those recommendations in sub-chapter VII (a) – *Tethered Currency*, and those directing their debt towards building infrastructure yielding future returns. For example, Angola, with a debt-to-*GDP* ratio of 111%, has oil and gas reserves of 9 billion barrels and 11 trillion cubic feet respectively. In addition, arable land covers 4% of its land mass, producing coffee and other crops, and forests 18% of land mass. Metals and minerals include iron ore, diamonds, and manganese. Djibouti, a country lacking natural resources, but which debt-to-*GDP* is 104%, have instead used debt to build infrastructure in integrated energy and petrochemicals facilities, refineries, railway lines, and electric power stations to support manufacturing in the production of steel, *PVC* pipes and glass.

High country-debt is most menacing when not supported by revenues from assets and used to provide future benefits.

Debt in so many countries is so huge that it, given the savings capacity of its citizens, cannot be repaid. Investors and countries holding debt are finally waking up to this reality, which will ultimately have them holding the bag. Debt forgiveness, also referred to as debt jubilee, according to Dr. Michael Hudson in his book . . . *and Forgive Them Their Debts: Lending, Foreclosure and Redemption From Bronze Age to the Jubilee Year*, says that debt forgiveness was practiced in the oldest civilizations on Earth, starting with Sumer, during the third millennium BC. The rulers then forgave debt on special occasions, such as the ascendancy of a leader, or the aftermath of a war, referred to as jubilee, for the purpose of keeping people out of bondage and slavery, and to limit the growth in power of the oligarchy class, a potential threat to the ruling elite. People in bondage were not available to partake in wars or serve as corvée labor, undermining the functioning of society. These were mainly farmers, in societies that were basically agrarian, who were indebted not necessarily through the issuance of loans, but who were unable to pay their obligations including fees and taxes owed the palace. Commercial loans issued to the merchant class were exempted from the debt jubilee.

Debt jubilees were opposed by the creditor class and started to dissipate during the Roman and Greek Empires. So today it is unthinkable that creditors would lend funds with a high risk of not receiving back those funds with interest. But that is exactly what happened to the creditors of Argentina debt, in 2002 after a default. Negotiations with bondholders, dragged on until June 2005, when the Argentina's President, Nestor Kirchner, made a final offer of exchanging old bonds for ones which were 25% of their value. 76% of the bondholders accepted the offer, a depreciation of 75% of their loans value.

Could Argentina's bond default happen to the US or other developed countries which print their currencies. The recent reaction of creditors to the UK increasing its deficits is revealing. Although the UK would not default on its debt because it would simply print the funds to cover due loans, creditors are finding other ways to express their disapproval. The Truss administration had proposed tax cuts and energy subsidies in the face of 9.1% consumer inflation, which budget measures would have not only impacted the general price level but also the debt-to-*GDP* ratio. At the same time, the Central Bank was tightening to address the near double-digit inflation. By demanding higher interest rates, external investors were driving bond prices down affecting pension funds dependent on prices of those bonds, which were then forced to sell more bonds increasing the supply on the market. With so much supply on the market, the external creditors were able to call the shots on interest rates.

The market reacted, causing the pound, the *UK* currency, to fall, and both the Prime Minister and Chancellor of the Exchequer lost their jobs as their term in office was shortened to a few weeks. The government was forced to reverse most of its budget proposals to have calm return to the market. The free-ride was over for the *UK*, a developed country with a debt-to-*GDP* ratio not yet exceeding 100%.

Was this unique to the *UK*, a country not dissimilar to the *US*? They both have large, chronic deficits in their government budgets (estimated by the IMF at around 4% of *GDP* for 2022), and their current accounts, the measure of trade in goods and services, investment income and transfers (estimated at 4.8% for the *UK* and 3.9%, *US*). At least Claudia Sahm, a former *Federal Reserve* economist, thinks that the *UK* financial crisis was not unique, and told a news website that Britain "is the canary in the coal mine."[24] Only time will reveal whether creditors have misplaced confidence in the *G7* developed nations defaulting on loans with great losses to them. The *UK* episode has demonstrated that a country's ability to print its currency will not be enough to save it from the market penalty of increasing unsustainable deficits and debt.

In summary, Baby Boomers and Generation X have left horrendous debt burdens for the younger generations that they cannot cope with. Countries have avoided defaulting on these debts by having their central banks manipulate the nominal interest rate to levels close to zero and

24 https://www.semafor.com/article/10/20/2022/theres-a-canary-in-the-coal-mine-for-the-us-in-the-uk-economic-fiasco?utm_source=flipboard&utm_content=user%2FSemafor

where the real interest rate is negative. But as investors, especially the external creditors, driven by ignorance or greed, realize their folly and that they are the ones that will bear the consequences of these defaults, this reckless behavior will come to a screeching halt as witnessed in the 2022 financial crisis in the *UK*. Debt jubilees will be the only solution and the slate will be wiped clean as with our ancestors.

With a clean slate, nations can take corrective actions and set new rules on debt. The lesson here is that going forward, debt should mainly be used to fund educational, capital, real estate, and infrastructural developments with future returns justifying it. And creditors who violate this straightforward rule should not anticipate any relief when the outcomes are not consistent with their expectations.

VII (D) – REDUCING INCOME AND WEALTH INEQUALITY

From the beginning, human societies have always been unequal with kings enjoying the benefits of serfs' labor, and rulers and aristocrats that of peasants. The wealthy lived in grand and comfortable structures while their servants in cramped and leaky huts. In medieval Europe, the dominant system was feudalism, where peasants paid homage to the nobleman, provided him with labor and a share of the produce from the land he allowed them to occupy and cultivate. The peasants and their families had high mortality rates and low life expectancies compared to their masters. As Adam Smith observed, "in the Highlands of Scotland for a mother who has borne twenty children not to have two alive."[25] Hospitals were founded as mass institutions for the poor as the rich could afford private home visits from their physicians. Societies are pyramidal in

---

25 https://quod.lib.umich.edu/cgi/t/text/pageviewer-idx?cc=ecco;c=ecco;idno=004861571
.0001.001;node=004861571.0001.001:5.8;seq=108;page=root;view=text

construct with the wealthy occupying the top echelons and everyone else the tiers below them. Wealth inequality is not a new phenomenon. But when these structures become too repressive for the masses, they have revolted to bring about some semblance of balance. Within the last several centuries, there have been three major revolutions – the French at the end of the 18th century, the Russian during the start of the 20th century and the Chinese at mid-20th century. The causes of the French revolution are thought to have been its regressive tax system (noblemen and clergy were exempted from taxation), food shortages resulting in starvation in the rural areas and inflation in urban centers, and high cost to service debt which stood at 55.6% of *GDP*. These problems reinforced the country's social and economic inequality, which came to a head with Queen Marie-Antoinette's contemptuous comment of *"let them eat cake"*. The French revolution resulted in the monarchy being abolished. The Russian revolution had similar origins. During *WWI*, Russia, one of the combatants, had printed large amounts of its currency to finance the war effort leading to hyper-inflation in the country. Farmers faced with higher cost of living but not commensurate increases in income, started to hoard their grain resulting in food shortages in cities. Workers started demanding higher wages in factories and participating in revolutionary parties. It was these revolutionary parties, such as the Bolsheviks, which led the revolution and once again the monarchy was overthrown and abolished. Three decades later, a similar revolution took place in China. Much of this time and from 1921 after the Chinese Communist Party was formed to advocate for land reform for the peasantry and organize among the urban workers, there was conflict with the Republic-of-China's army leading to the civil war of 1945 to 1949. The defeated Republic-of-China's army retreated to Taiwan and the Chinese Communist Party assumed control of China. Some historians identify the distinct inequalities that existed during the early twentieth century as an important factor for the revolution. High rents, usury, and taxes collectively led to a concentration of wealth in the hands of a minority of village chiefs and landlords. Revolutions were the means these countries used to bring about more equal societies.

In our present era, the possibility of a popular uprising along the lines of the French, Russian and Chinese revolutions is rare. Although there is still significant inherited wealth as existed in the past, societies have changed, and the kingship form of governing has largely been abandoned or given a superficial role in the decision-making of nations. More citizens now have a say in how and by whom they are ruled. But wealth inequality remains and may have gotten worse, not from the toils of labor, but due to market power and the unnecessary meddling of central banks in their economies. Some of the wealthiest individuals have attained their status from companies they formed with limited or no competition as they remain either monopolies or oligopolies. Companies like the electric car company, Tesla, the online retail store, Amazon, and the social media platform, Facebook. And then there are central banks in developed countries increasing the money supply of those countries for purposes of growing their *GDP* but instead unwittingly increasing inequality from asset bubbles. The owners of these assets, including stocks, bonds, and real estate, are already people of substantial means and the banks *Quantitative Easing* measures increase their value. They also use the cheap money from *Quantitative Easing* to leverage companies and real estate purchases. Further, companies have been buying back their stock with cheap money, pushing the price of the stock upwards with executives benefiting from compensation packages tied to the performance of their stock.

But Plato, the fourth century *BCE* Greek philosopher, proposed a viable solution to the income inequality problem. Plato believed that the income of the highest paid in society should never amount to more than five times that of the lowest paid. This accomplishes two things. It limits the income of those with market power and increases the incomes of the lowest paid for the highest paid to receive higher compensation. If Mr. Bezos paid his workers $15/hour and he wanted to earn $100/

hour, he would need to increase his workers' wages to $20 under Plato's formula. However, it does not decrease inequality as the highest paid income increases by multiples, in this case five times, that of the lowest paid. So, if the lowest paid income increases by one unit of currency, the highest increases by five units, thereby expanding the absolute difference. Although it makes no sense to stifle innovation by placing caps on income as Plato recommends, some sort of bifurcation of income is needed to address income inequality which leads to wealth inequality. The bifurcation can be for tax purposes. So, a proposal could be for setting an upper income level comparable to Plato's 5 times, which could be whatever a country decides is just and would not retard innovation, let's say, 20 times, but all income earned above that level by any individual would be taxed at a much higher rate, say 75%. Part of the additional tax revenues would then be used for income-support programs to the lowest-income members of the society. But to avoid expanding income inequality due to the effect of the multiplier, as explained above, the upper limit, once set, should be maintained in place for some period of time, perhaps years times a multiplier. Using Plato's multiplier would yield five years.

VII (E) – POPULATION CONTROL

The case was made in sub-chapter VI (b) *Symptoms of Economic Destruction, Environmental Degradation,* that the planet is overpopulated causing destruction and death from climate change and with little or no effort to change its course. The destruction and death are the Malthusian explanation to the imbalance from the overpopulation. But we should not have to wait for natural corrections for what is man-made. In the developed countries, social and economic changes are resulting in lower fertility rates, a major determinant of population growth. These changes include the need for both parents to work to maintain the family due to the high cost-of-living in developed countries, the empowerment of women in both education and the workforce, the widespread availability of contraception, and the high cost of rearing children. But not so in some developing countries, especially in Africa. Although fertility rates for the world have been halved since 1960, which means that its population is increasing but at a slower rate of growth, sub-Saharan Africa only decreased by 30% from 6.60 to 4.56, as shown in **Figure 32**. But natural phenomena such as droughts are taking a toll especially in East Africa.

In 2022, there was much anguish associated with families, trekking from drought regions in search of food, and burying their children along the route who had died from hunger. This is one of the ways the planet restores equilibrium to its limited resources and the demand and use of those resources.

The comparison to the fertility rates of developed countries such as North America and the European Union is stark and consistent with declining populations. These societies have fertility rates less than 2.00,

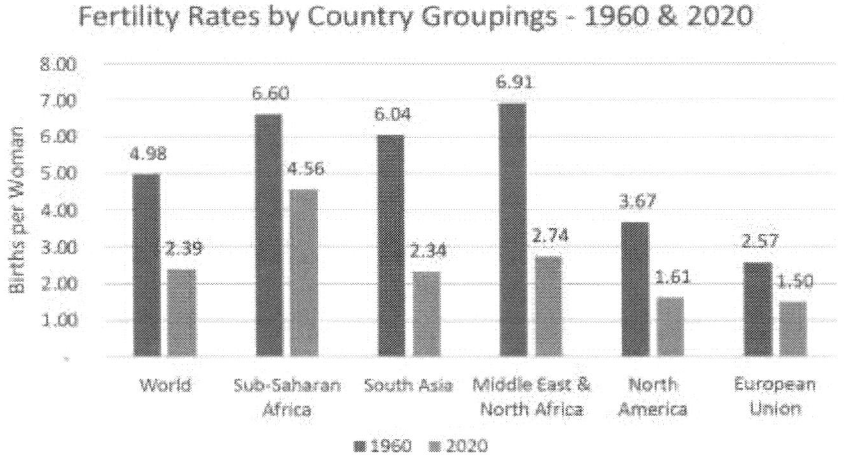

Fertility Rates by Country Groupings - 1960 & 2020

Figure 32

Source: **World Bank**

146

a level which is theoretically associated with a constant rate of growth, due to replacement mortality. The rationale is that for every two children born in a family, they replace their parents as they eventually die. But decreases in fertility and population levels are not contemporaneous, and population changes follow fertility changes by several decades, some 40 to 50 years later. Japan's fertility rate in 1960 was 2.0 but its population took several decades to show decline and in 2021, 61 years later, its population level is now the same as it was in 1996, 125.8 million. Japan's population decline started around 2011 at 128.1 million. One can make the case that the 1960 fertility rate had an impact on population growth 50 years later in 2011, when the decline started. The fertility rate in the *US*, another developed country, has been declining since 1960 when it stood at 3.65, but its population has not followed the trend. The aberration in population growth in the *US* compared to Japan can likely be contributed to migration, a country more welcoming to migrants than Japan.

The country data is supported by income data. Developed countries have lower fertility rates because of the reasons mentioned above, mainly due to more women entering the labor force and choosing careers over homemaking. The income data (**Figure 33**) show that for both high-income and upper middle-income countries, fertility rates are below 2.0, a sign that their populations growth rates are declining. On the other hand, low-income and *Highly Indebted Poor Countries (HIPC)* have fertility rates way above the 2.0 level, an indication of substantial population growth. Large populations will continue to keep these countries poor and stagnate their efforts to improve the wellbeing of their people.

And no one in the African and low-income countries are proposing solutions to the problem of population size. It may not be on their radar as a problem. In the *US*, there are wrong-headed proposals to provide parents of children with more income support. Besides being misguided to have taxpayers subsidize the decision-making of couples to grow their

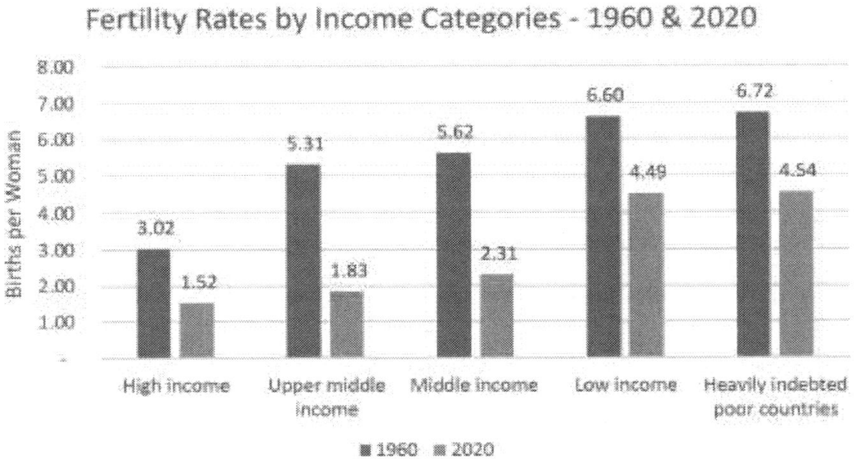

Fertility Rates by Income Categories - 1960 & 2020

Figure 33

Source: **World Bank**

families, income support to them will only increase their numbers as it mitigates one of the reason societies have lower fertility rates, the high cost of living.

Although the Chinese solution of one child per family is not the preferred approach due to its imposed manner of implementation, its goals were laudable. Further, because it was imposed, the policy didn't seem to have had achieved its goals and China's fertility rates were never below 1.6, a low which occurred between 1998 and 2003. Instead, countries with high fertility and population growth rates, which we have seen are low-income and designated *High Indebted Poor Countries (HIPC)*, should be given monetary incentives to educate their populations on the benefits for reducing family size, to educate their female citizens, and to make contraceptives widely available to the general population. Some may argue that an education campaign is slow, which may have merit, but it allows citizens to buy-in to the policy and therefore become a devoted supporter. And, as already demonstrated, reducing fertility rates is also slow, taking several decades to show results.

Further, there is a need for voluntary euthanasia in each country. Currently, of the almost 200 nations, only a handful, mainly in Europe such as Belgium, the Netherlands, Luxembourg, and Spain, permit voluntary euthanasia. The procedure allows terminally ill patients and those who see no value in continuing their lives, to bring an end to living. Besides voluntary, there is no need to provide extraordinary means to persons in a vegetable state to stay alive, incurring large healthcare costs with no benefit. It is time to let those who want to leave get their intentions fulfilled, and those who are not able to decide, have some capable persons, such as medical personnel or close family members, make that decision for them.

From a combination of overpopulation and technology substitution, countries will no longer be able to provide full employment for their workers. A phenomenon developed over the past few decades is that of older workers continuing to work although their productivity has been affected by decreases in energy levels and mental acuity. Employers would naturally want to replace these workers with younger more productive workers but are prevented from doing so by the fear of being accused of age discrimination. Before, companies had policies on mandatory retirement ages, but workers are no longer forced to retire at a certain age but are allowed to do so at their volition and discretion. This is obviously affecting the employment and promotion of younger workers and is one of the ailments of our economies. To correct, companies should be given the right to set retirement ages for their workers without facing court challenges and providing this policy is applied in an indiscriminatory manner, across all levels of employment.

CHAPTER SUMMARY

This chapter deals with the existential macroeconomic problems facing the developed and other countries and the difficult decisions needed to extricate their economies from the pending destruction. The chief culprits are fiat currency and excessive debt. These in turn affect the depreciation of currencies and concentrate wealth in the hands of a few. Corrective action will not come easily as many have their self-interest served by such a system.

The solution involves four major changes. The first is the abolition of fiat currency where governments proclaim paper money as legal tender, and give each country's money intrinsic value, backed by transferable assets of each country. These assets can be of three categories with value in providing metals, minerals, and energy in the production process, protecting forests and other carbon-capturing natural phenomena from destruction by the issuance of carbon credits, and utilizing arable land to produce food. All countries have wealth, and their currencies would reflect those levels of wealth. Such a system with a one-world currency divided among countries based on each asset pool will eliminate some of the bad apples in the barrel. For countries using the universal currency for domestic exchanges, as they can only increase their money supply, the definition of inflation, from discovery of new resources or revalue of assets from market changes, asset inflation will disappear. Consumer inflation is possible from the improper use of debt but is self-correcting as future income already expended is not available leading to a correcting recession. Under the current system, the central bank would prime the economy with lower interest rates and *Quantitative Easing*. But the role of central banks will change in the new dispensation and will be limited, ensuring that member commercial banks have sufficient liquidity, and act as the depository for all customers eliminating the occasional future bank runs and bankruptcies. The same self-correcting action is applicable to trade deficits as outflows of currency to pay for the higher level of imports, will reduce countries' reserves and cause depreciation of local currencies.

Debt, used to support operating costs, is a major concern for many countries but as mentioned above is self-correcting with a world currency system backed by assets. But what's to become of all that public debt which cannot be repaid. Colloquially, creditors will have to take a haircut. This could be quite disrupting to the world's economy as several Countries own bonds of other countries and would have to accept less than par value for the debt.

And how will income and wealth inequality fare with the elimination of fiat currency? It has already been demonstrated that some of the inequality is created by central banks lowering interest rates and increasing the money supply to asset holders, already the wealthy in society, but that wealth creation will disappear as the role of the central banks will have to change. These banks can only manipulate the money supply in a fiat currency environment, not an environment where currencies are backed by assets. As a result, not only will there be a better distribution of income among society and consequently an increase in demand, but the constraint would decrease the growing misery people are experiencing worldwide. This misery and pain are not apparent as it is easily masked by increases in *GDP*. The New York Times correspondent, David Brooks, in this article *The Rising Tide of Global Sadness*[26], recently admitted being surprised to learn that countries like India and China were experiencing high levels of misery despite healthy growth in their *GDP*s. The condition was attributed to widening inequality. An annual Gallup survey of 150,000 people in 140 countries, showing negative emotions related to stress, sadness, anger, worry and physical pain, hit a record high in 2021. Although some inequality is desirable to encourage innovation, that which is not associated with renewal and invention, such as that created by increasing the money supply, would be eliminated and an

---

26 https://www.nytimes.com/2022/10/27/opinion/global-sadness-rising.html

appropriate amount of what remains should be used as transfer payments to improve the lives of citizens.

VIII

NOTES

Notes appearing in this section are not necessarily references to support content in the book but also tidbits the readership may find insighful of a particular event, expert, or analyst. The history of our great thinkers is so little known that it should be refreshing to know more about those that made improvements in our lives which for the most part is taken for granted as our societies concentrate on 'bread and circus' activities associated with ancient decay and destruction (Ross Douthat, opinion columnist at the New York Times, rebranded this metaphor of decay "pot and circuses" in an article *Five theses on the future of liberalism*, and in an attempt to be more relevant to the times). People now tenc to worship at the altar of the 'celebrity', an actor, comedian, or sports participant; compensate them far beyond the benefits offered while ignoring those spreading knowledge and improving our lives through inventions. For example, a sports personality, who makes a career out of an activity with high recreational utility, sports and games, is paid far more than our teachers who transfers knowledge to students, creating and improving the human capital the economy needs to grow. Economics justifies compensation for work because of its disutility, but here it is turned on its head and society super compensates for utility, not disutility. At least in ancient societies where 'bread and circus' were symptoms of decadence, the circus/sports usually resulted in someone losing his life, such as a gladiator, a great disutility to participate.

So, people like Sir John Harrington, who invented the flush toilet, thereby gradually replacing the medieval practice of emptying human waste out of

153

windows and into streets requiring the hiring of muck-rackers to keep the streets walkable, is little known. That's an improvement to the human condition taken for granted with little or no recognition for Harrington. But we need to recognize those with superficial impacts on our lives are part of the decadence taking place in our societies and not unlike that coming from the political economy discussed above. Both give the false perception of feel-good while having a contrary effect.

VIII (A) – INTRODUCTION

Links to Louis Holder's published articles on *The Future Begins Now*, in Stabroek News Business Weekly at https://www.stabroeknews.com.

VIII (B) – CHAPTER I (POLITICAL ECONOMY)

Reference of kingship being given human civilization by our Gods, although meant for levity, is supported by Sumerian/Acadian/Assyrian/Babylonian cuneiform tablets which narrative is documented in Zecharia Sitchin series *Earth Chronicles*. In brief, and according to Sitchin, Extraterrestrials from Planet Nibiru, a planet referred to by Caltech's scientists as Planet 9, in a 10,000-year orbit in our solar system, visited Earth. Its inhabitants came here to extract gold and would enter/exit Earth as their planet approached/left. Having created Homo Sapiens from Homo Erectus using genetic engineering, and for the purpose of slave labor, the Gods decided to allow Homo Sapiens self-rule over 8,000 years ago in Sumer, Mesopotamia.

VIII (C) – CHAPTER II (THE THEORISTS)

Adam Smith

Adam Smith believed in unfettered markets for the supply of and demand for labor and condemned efforts by the authorities to come down harshly on Labor Unions while turning a blind eye to similar employer action.

"We rarely hear, it has been said, of the combinations of masters, though frequently of those of workmen. But whoever imagines, upon this account, that masters rarely combine, is as ignorant of the world as of the subject. Masters are always and everywhere in a sort of tacit, but constant and uniform, combination, not to raise the wages of labour above their actual rate [. . .] Masters, too, sometimes enter into particular combinations to sink the wages of labour even below this rate. These are always conducted with the utmost silence and secrecy till the moment of execution; and when the workmen yield, as they sometimes do without resistance, though severely felt by them, they are never heard of by other people". In contrast, when workers combine, "the masters [. . .] never cease to call aloud for the assistance of the civil magistrate, and the rigorous execution of those laws which have been enacted with so much severity against the combination of servants, labourers, and journeymen." (Book 1, chapter Viii)

Smith was well aware of the poverty and children mortality of the times. "poverty, though it does not prevent the generation, is extremely unfavourable to the rearing of children [. . .] It is not uncommon [. . .] in the Highlands of Scotland for a mother who has borne twenty children not to have two alive [. . .] In some places one half the children born die before they are four years of age; in many places before they are seven; and in almost all places before they are nine or ten. This great mortality, however, will every where be found chiefly among the children of the common people, who cannot afford to tend them with the same care as those of better station." (Book 1, chapter Viii, para 37).

The stock referred to here by Smith is obviously savings from labor. In this sense, he is clearly on the same page as Marx, who holds that capital is the accumulation of labor. "When the stock which a man possesses is no more than sufficient to maintain him for a few days or a few weeks, he seldom thinks of deriving any revenue from it. He consumes it as sparingly as he can, and endeavours by his labour to acquire something which may supply its place before it be consumed altogether. His revenue is, in this case, derived from his labour only. This is the state of the greater part of the labouring poor in all countries.

But when he possesses stock sufficient to maintain him for months or years, he naturally endeavours to derive a revenue from the greater part of it; reserving only so much for his immediate consumption as may maintain him till this revenue begins to come in. His whole stock, therefore, is distinguished into two parts. That part which, he expects, is to afford him this revenue, is called his capital". (Book 2, chapter i, para 1–2).

Smith is best known for his *Invisible Hand* metaphor but only uses it once in explaining how free markets promote the public interest. "As every individual, therefore, endeavours as much as he can both to employ his capital in the support of domestic industry, and so to direct that industry that its produce may be of the greatest value; every individual necessarily labours to render the annual revenue of the society as great as he can. He generally, indeed, neither intends to promote the public interest, nor knows how much he is promoting it. By preferring the support of domestic to that of foreign industry, he intends only his own security; and by directing that industry in such a manner as its produce may be of the greatest value, he intends only his own gain, and he is in this, as in many other cases, led by an *invisible hand* to promote an end which was no part of his intention. Nor is it always the worse for the society that it was no part of it. By pursuing his own interest he frequently promotes that of the society more effectually than when he really intends to promote it." (Book 4, Chapter 2]

Smith understood that free markets, although the best option at the national level, did not bring about desirable outcomes for all its people. These markets will not eradicate poverty. He therefore saw a role for governments to correct this imbalance through a progressive tax system. "The necessaries of life occasion the great expense of the poor. They find it difficult to get food, and the greater part of their little revenue is spent in getting it. The luxuries and vanities of life occasion the principal expense of the rich, and a magnificent house embellishes and sets off to the best advantage all the other luxuries and vanities which they possess. A tax upon house-rents, therefore, would in general fall heaviest upon the rich; and in this sort of inequality there would not, perhaps, be anything very unreasonable. It is not very unreasonable that the rich should contribute to the public expense, not only in proportion to their revenue, but something more than in that proportion" (Book 5, Chapter ii, Article 1).

This prescience observation is more correct today than during the 18th century and is responsible for the unsustainable large debts of Nations. ". . . when war comes [politicians] are both unwilling and unable to increase their [tax] revenue in proportion to the increase of their expense. They are unwilling for fear of offending the people, who, by so great and so sudden an increase of taxes, would soon be disgusted with the war [. . .] The facility of borrowing delivers them from the embarrassment [. . .] By means of borrowing they are enabled, with a very moderate increase of taxes, to raise, from year to year, money sufficient for carrying on the war, and by the practice of perpetually funding they are enabled, with the smallest possible increase of taxes [to pay the interest on the debt], to raise annually the largest possible sum of money [to fund the war].   The return of peace, indeed, seldom relieves them from the greater part of the taxes imposed during the war. These are mortgaged for the interest of the debt contracted in order to carry it on." (Book 5, Chapter iii, Article 3)

Thomas Richard Malthus

Malthus postulated that, in support for population control, "If the subsistence for man that the earth affords was to be increased every twenty-five years by a quantity equal to what the whole world at present produces, this would allow the power of production in the earth to be absolutely unlimited, and its ratio of increase much greater than we can conceive that any possible exertions of mankind could make it, yet still the power of population being a power of a superior order, the increase of the human species can only be kept commensurate to the increase of the means of subsistence by the constant operation of the strong law of necessity acting as a check upon the greater power." (Malthus T. R. 1798. *An Essay on the Principle of Population.* Chapter 2, p. 8). In sketching the argument of his theory on population Malthus wrote "Assuming then my postulate as granted, I say, that the power of population is indefinitely greater than the power in the Earth to produce subsistence for Man."

"Population, when unchecked, increases at a geometric ratio. Subsistence increases only in an arithmetical ration. A slight acquaintance with numbers will shew the immensity of the first power in comparison of the second."

"By the law of nature which makes food necessary to the life of man, the effects of these two unequal powers must be kept equal."

"This implies a strong and constantly operating check on population from the difficulty of subsistence. This difficulty must fall somewhere and must necessarily be severely felt by a large portion of mankind" (Malthus T. R., *An Essay on the Principles of Population*, p. 9)

Malthus was not supportive of the poor laws of England for in his opinion it worsened the condition of the poor. England's Poor Bill allowed a shilling a week to every laborer for each child above 3. Malthus opposed it as it made no provision to increase produce thus the same provision would be spread over a larger population increased by the subsidy. "Mr. Pitt's Poor Bill has the appearance of being framed with benevolent intentions, and the clamour raised against it in many respects ill directed, and unreasonable. But it must be confessed that it possesses in a high degree the great and radical defect of all systems of the kind, that the tending to increase population without increasing the means for its support, and thus to depress the condition of those that are not supported by parishes, and consequently, to create more poor." (Malthus T. R., *An Essay on the Principles of Population*, p. 38)

Malthus' 3 propositions on population: 1. Population cannot increase without the means of subsistence. 2. Population does invariably increase where there are the means of subsistence, and 3. The superior power of population cannot be checked without producing misery or vice. (Malthus T. R., *An Essay on the Principles of Population*, p. 18)

Malthus identified his great checks to population as 1. Proper and sufficient food supply. 2. Hard labor and unwholesome habitations, followed by his preventative and positive checks of. 3. Vicious customs with respect to women. 4. Great cities. 5. Unwholesome manufacturers. 6. Luxury. 7. Pestilence, and 8. War. (Malthus T. R., *An Essay on the Principles of Population*, p. 39)

Malthus's thought reflects a reaction, amiably conducted, to his father's views and to the doctrines of the French Revolution and its supporters, such as the English radical philosopher William Godwin. Widely read for such works as *Political Justice* (1793), Godwin took for granted the perfectibility of humankind and looked to a millennium in which rational people would live prosperously and harmoniously without laws and institutions. Unlike Godwin (or, earlier, Rousseau), who viewed human affairs from a theoretical standpoint, Malthus was essentially an empiricist and took as his starting point the harsh realities of his time. His reaction developed in the tradition of British economics, which would today be considered sociological. (Britannica, *Thomas Malthus, English economist and demographer*)

Malthus continued publishing a variety of pamphlets and tracts on economics. In an approach less rigorous than Ricardo's, he discussed the problem of price determination in terms of an institutionally determined "effective demand," a phrase that he invented. In his summary *Principles of Political Economy Considered with a View to Their Practical Application* (1820), Malthus went so far as to propose public works and private luxury investment as possible solutions for economic distress through their ability to increase demand and prosperity. He criticized those who valued thrift as a virtue knowing no limit; to the contrary, he argued that "the principles of saving, pushed to excess, would destroy the motive to production." To maximize wealth, a nation had to balance "the power to produce and the will to consume." In fact, Malthus, as an economist concerned with what he called the problem of "gluts" (or, as they would be called today, the problems of economic recession or depression), can be said to have anticipated the economic discoveries made by the English

159

economist John Maynard Keynes in the 1930s. (Britannica, *Thomas Malthus, English economist and demographer*)

Malthus differentiated between nominal and real price of labor and how the fall in real price benefits farmers and capitalists "It very rarely happens that the nominal price of labor universally falls, but we well know that it frequently remains the same, while the nominal price of provisions has been gradually increasing. This is, in effect, a real fall in the price of labor, and during this period the condition of the lower orders of the community must gradually grow worst and worst. But the farmers and capitalists are growing rich from the real cheapness of labor." (Malthus T. R., *An Essay on the Principles of Population*, p.16)

Karl Marx

Marx was born into a family which had converted from Judaism to Christianity but had become an Atheist. His understanding of religion as preserving the status quo of inequality is captured in this passage: "Religious suffering is, at one and the same time, the expression of real suffering and a protest against real suffering. Religion is the sigh of the oppressed creature, the heart of a heartless world, and the soul of soulless conditions. It is the opium of the people. The abolition of religion as the illusory happiness of the people is the demand for their real happiness. To call on them to give up their illusions about their condition is to call on them to give up a condition that requires illusions." (*Critique of Hegel's Philosophy of Right*, p. 131)

Marx recognized that there were benefits offered by *capitalism* such as increases in productivity and growth, responsible for societal progress compared to earlier forms such as feudalism. He considered the capitalist class to be one of the most revolutionary in history because it constantly improved the means of production more so than any other class and was responsible for the overthrow of feudalism. But features of exploitation and recurring cyclical depressions, leading to mass unemployment, more than offset the benefits.

The exploitation came from the capitalist taking advantage of surplus value, the difference between unit-costs of inputs and outputs, or the difference between what it costs to keep workers alive and what they produce. The instability leading to mass employment came from the system being prone to periodic crisis because the capitalists invested more in new technologies and less in labor. As profit was the surplus value extracted from labor, the decline in labor would result in the rate of profit decreasing causing growth to collapse. In Marx's communist society, exploitation would end, and workers would not be bound to sell their labor. He saw this society as stateless as the State previously served to enforce the exploitation. The transition from *capitalism* to *communism* would be filled for a period by a dictatorship of the proletariat or workers, which for countries with strong democratic institutions such as Britain, the United States and the Netherlands, would be peaceful. Others would require the force of revolutions.

John Maynard Keynes

Keynes took a leadership role in the mid-1944s in the World Bank Commission charged with establishing a new world financial system which was subsequently referred to as the *Bretton Woods Agreement*. Keynes' proposal was for the creation of an international clearing-union, a common world currency, and a world central bank (*WCB*) to manage the entire system. Keynes' proposal is not unlike the proposals made by the Author of this book, the major difference being that Keynes didn't see the need for this currency to be asset backed, depending on the discipline of the *WCB*. In hindsight, Keynes' proposal was superior to that of the Americans, but the USA's greater negotiating strength carried the day. The plan adopted was for the *US* dollar to be the world reserve currency backed by gold priced at $35 per ounce.

In a new book, *Money & Empire: Charles P. Kindleberger and the Dollar System*, by Perry Mehrling, it was revealed that Charles Kindleberger, an MIT economist, proposed a one world currency, the U.S. dollar. He argued that there would be more trade, cross-border investment, and prosperity if all nations either adopted dollars or tied their currencies to the dollar at a fixed exchange rate, which has almost the same effect. Further, the dollar system he envisioned would not run on autopilot, nor would it be free of travail. "Such a world will be full of ambiguity, paradox, uncertainty and problems," he wrote. Thus, supporting a world central banker.

Keynes' remedy for economic downturns is government deficit spending with offsetting surpluses after the economy had recovered and was growing again. Keynesian economists were able to demonstrate an inverse relationship between unemployment and inflation, referred to as the Phillips curve. As unemployment increase, the economy loses demand and consumer inflation decreases. But in the 1970s, during the oil embargo, both unemployment and inflation increased, which would happen if supply fell below the declining demand from the higher unemployment. The critics of Keynesian economics seized on the moment to make the case that it is not supported, that the relationship between unemployment and inflation does not exist. The monetarists, headed by Milton Friedman, are not supportive of fiscal policy for solving economic problems and thus are not supportive of Keynes policies. The monetarists feel that a better outcome can be achieved by manipulating the money supply and interest rate. President Harry S. Truman was a sceptic of Keynesian theorizing, saying: "Nobody can ever convince me that government can spend a dollar that it's not got."

Deng Xiaoping

Karl Marx saw *communism* as the ultimate stage of evolution which had to have experienced *capitalism* before. Deng Xiaoping appears to have embraced this position by introducing market forces in the Chinese economy for it to be able to evolve to a Communist State.

Milton Friedman

Friedman's economic thinking changed over time as he was supportive of FDR's New Deal measures to stimulate the economy, from which he benefitted directly through employment. The creation of jobs through public works and work relief program were all fiscal programs intended to take workers off the bread line and provide them instead with employment. Then, as a Treasury spokesman during 1942, he advocated a Keynesian policy of taxation, another fiscal approach, as a way of raising taxes to fund the war. Later, he argued that the New Deal was not the right solution for the Great Depression, which was caused by a severe monetary contraction due to banking crises and poor policy on the part of the *Fed*. And he became a fierce critic of Keynes.

Friedman was the main proponent of monetary policy associated with the Chicago School of Economics where he taught for 30 years. He theorized that there is a close and stable association between inflation and the money supply, and that inflation could be avoided with proper regulation of the growth in the money supply. This is the central planning approach used by Central Banks around the World but as already pointed out in the book, manipulation of the money supply leads to asset inflation and not changes to the *CPI*.

Friedman rejected the use of Keynesian fiscal policy as a tool to manage demand and held that this should fall within the realm of monetary policy.

Friedman served the *US* Ronald Reagan as an unofficial advisor and consulted with *UK* Margaret Thatcher due to his support of free-markets and small governments. But unlike Richard Nixon who proclaimed to be a Keynesian, Reagan made no such association and instead honored him with the Presidential Medal of Freedom.

VIII (D) – CHAPTER III (STAKEHOLDERS)

Households

According to PEW Research Center, in 2014, some 29% of all mothers living with children younger than 18 are at home with their children. This is an increase from 1999, when it was 23%, and probably the result of lack of employment opportunities (over a longer period, 1960 to 2014, stay-at-home moms actually declined by about 20%, suggesting a recent reversal). As family structures with stay-at-home mothers are generally less well off than working mothers in terms of education and income, household incomes are being affected by this recent trend. The median household income for families with a stay-at-home mom and a full-time working dad was $55,000 in 2014, roughly half the median income for families in which both parents work full-time ($102,400). Other trends, such as children living in single-parent arrangements, are up from 9% in 1960 to 26% in 2014, and those living with natural parents, which are down from 73% to 46% over the same period, portends the lowering of incomes from this sector. This is driving the despair discussed in Chapter VI (e) as lower household incomes from the loss of middle-class jobs are causing workers to forego marriage and the rearing of children.

Commerce

If commerce is the research and activity to promote job creation and sustainable economic growth in meeting the demands of society, where would the growth come from when needs are being met through production and net imports? Innovation! And according to KPMG's 2018 global technology innovation survey, more than a third of technology-industry leaders globally say the U.S. remains the world's leading technology and innovation hub. Technological advances over the past twenty years include expansion of broadband services coupled with mobile phones and the internet of things, the growth in social media platforms with Facebook alone having 2.26 billion users, advancements in curbs to greenhouse gas emissions through plant-based meats and electric vehicles, among others. Unfortunately, many of the innovations are designed to substitute for labor causing its displacement.

Investors

Households are heavily invested in capital markets through retirement funds amounting to $26.4 trillion in the second quarter of 2022, 31% of all household financial assets. A breakdown of the total retirement investment is as follows: Individual Retirement Accounts (IRAs) $11.7 trillion; Defined Contribution

(DC) $9.3 trillion; Private-sector defined-benefit (DB) retirement plans $3.2 trillion; and Annuity Reserves outside of retirement accounts $2.2 trillion. The value of these assets is subject to the vagaries of the *Fed* in its manipulation of the money supply and the resulting inflationary effects. The value of retirement assets declined by 10.2% between March 31 and June 30, 2022, due to the *Fed* raising interest rates to reduce general inflation (S&P 500 decreased 16% during the same period). It is estimated that 67% of retirement assets are invested in the stock market.

Governments

Empirical research shows that representative systems of governance tend to be biased towards the affluent classes and not the population in general. These representatives are not required to fulfill promises made to the electorate and instead promote their own self-interests once elected. The representation of these interests fosters inequality in society.

Further, according to OpenSecrets, a research group, data from lawmakers 2019 financial disclosures, shows the median net worth of members of Congress who filed disclosures was just over $1 million. Compared to the average American household which real asset value increased by 3.7% from 2004 to 2012, the increase for members on Congress was 15.4%. The *US Congress* is not only an exclusive club, but a wealthy one.

Central Banks

There is no scientific basis for the 2% inflation target that Central Banks in the *US*, Canada, European Union, *UK*, Japan, and other western countries follow. It is believed that it originated in New Zealand around 1988 as an off-the-cuff TV remark and subsequently, with some adjustments for upward bias, adopted by its country's finance minister, Roger Douglas. This spread through the central banking community as orthodoxy. The Central Bankers also wanted some wiggle room for addressing recessions by monetary policy which would have a better chance of success the higher the targeted inflation rate. The *US Fed* is now looking at 2%, not on an annual basis, but as an average over several years. Thus, in some years when actual inflation is below the target, other years can have their actuals above the target so the average of the block of years is 2%. This allows the *Fed* to increase its monetary stimulus practices to bring about higher growth in the economy without being constrained by the 2% annual target. The *US* has been using the 2% target since 1996 and explicitly since 2012.

In the June 21, 2022 edition of the New York Times, a prominent economist and columnist, Paul Krugman, posed the question that if the *Fed* was consistently setting the targeted interest below the natural rate of interest, rate consistent with price stability, where was the runaway inflation? In his answer, he cast doubt on the claim that the inflation was concentrated in the asset sector as there were other asset bubbles without low interest rates. The answer failed to recognize that the *Fed* keeps interest rates low by increasing its members' reserve margins which first go as loans to their large corporations and used by them to leverage their Companies through stock-buybacks. Stock-buybacks, once illegal in the *US*, promote stock price increases when interest rates are lower than stock returns. The lower rates also have an impact on real estate driving prices up as investors can pay more for the property because of the reduction in the rate of interest and stay within a specified total cost budget. So, asset bubbles may not have low interest rates as a requirement, but low interest rates will undoubtedly result in asset soaking up inflation.

The lowering of interest rates by the Central Bank has no impact on consumer credit card rates as these unsecured loans are impacted by delinquency rates and therefore have no stimulus effect on the *PCE* inflation rate, the *Fed* 2% target. When funds are given directly to consumers, as was the case of the pandemic relief in 2020 and 2021, demand is injected into the economy and consumer inflation takes off. It is a weakness with the *Fed* that it targets the *PCE* instead of asset inflation for the damaging effects its money supply measures are having on the economy.

VIII (E) – CHAPTER IV
(ECONOMIC PARAMETERS)

Price Inflation

Business cycles are expansions and contractions in an economy where expansions are characterized by price increases, which in turn reduces demand as consumers spending is curtailed by the higher prices. Contractions are of opposite attributes. Typically, expansions have a longer lifespan than recessions having been almost equal during the 1854–1899 period (27 months vs 24 months, respectively). The gap kept increasing and for the period 1982-2009, the gap had widened to 103:1, expansion to contraction. Many attribute this outcome to the management of the monetary economy by the *Fed*.

This outlook ignores the role of China's participation in the world economy acting as its manufacturer. China produced goods the World wanted at low prices and in exchange for its paper money. This is the only reasonable explanation given the expansionary fiscal and monetary policies of governments willing to tolerate large budget deficits and low interest rates.

Classical economists from the Austrian School, argue that business cycles are caused by excessive issuance of credit by banks in fractional reserve banking systems. The same effect comes about when central banks set interest rates too low, and the resulting expansion of the money supply causes a "boom" in which resources are misallocated and prices rise. Demand cannot be sustained in a rising price environment and a "bust" follows.

VIII (F) – CHAPTER V (COMPONENTS OF
ECONOMIC DESTRUCTION)

Fiat Currency

Although designated legal tender, there is no federal statute mandating that private businesses, persons, or organizations accept fiat currency as payment for goods or services. Private businesses are free to develop their own policies on the acceptance of cash subject to State Law. This has led businesses to reject cash as digital payments become more popular due to ease and increasing efficiency of transactions. But many consumers still have a preference for cash payment prompting, for example, New York State to pass a Law in 2019 that prohibits food service and retail establishments from refusing to accept cash as payment for goods or services and calls for a civil fine if an establishment should refuse cash as payment. According to the NYC Consumer Affairs, there are over 300,000 households in the City that are unbanked and would be isolated from those businesses if prohibited from using cash.

GDP Growth

GDP has limited usefulness as a measure of living standards for what it contains, for example rent-seeking and combating criminal activities, and the paucity of information it provides, such as income inequality. This improves with comparisons with GDP ratios such as real per-capita GDP. But, perhaps the most reflective ratio of living standards, intra- and inter-countries but not given widespread use, is per-capita purchase power parity (PPP) index.

PPP determines the cost of a basket of goods and services in terms of labor participation (the number of hours worked to afford the items). When the comparison is between time periods in a specific country, or among countries using their rate-adjusted exchange currencies, it provides a more accurate picture of well-being between periods or between countries. Yet since the mid-1940s (1991 for the US), countries have depended on GDP as the index of well-being in the World.

Inflation Targets

Many developed countries set their inflation targets at around 2%, but some countries, specifically African, have targets in the high single digit numbers. Liberia, Ghana, Nigeria, Egypt, and Zambia have targets ranging between 6% and 9%. For these countries, their cost-of-living will double in 8 and 12 years, with the resultant loss of labor competitiveness. On the positive side, their cost-of-living indices are below those of the developed countries, so although increasing at a more rapid rate, they still have a way to go before surpassing. Whereas developed countries at 2% inflation targets will take 35 years to double, these high-inflation countries will do so every 10 years and should be on par from where they are now, in a few decades.

Deficit-Causing Tax Cuts

Reagan tax cuts had the effect of expanding the debt from less than $1 trillion to almost $3 trillion during his administration, an unprecedented increase for that era. The administration was forced to pare back some of his tax cuts in 1984 to try and make up the budget shortfall. The group benefitting the most from these tax cuts were apparently the rich and the number of millionaires increased from 500,000 in 1980 to 900,000 by 1986.

VIII (G) – CHAPTER VI (SYMPTOMS OF ECONOMIC DESTRUCTION)

Environmental Degradation

Is all of the planet's climate change, man-made? Why is the progress of deterioration happening at what appears to be an exponential rate? There is another scientific explanation for environmental changes occurring which hasn't been given much exposure. Two scientists at the California Institute of Technology (Caltech), Pasadena, California, Messrs. Konstantin Batygin and Mike Brown, have theorized that a large planet in an elongated orbit of our solar system on what appears to be a 10,000-year orbit, is approaching resulting in the peculiar way objects are behaving in the Kuiper Belt. They have not located the planet yet and make no claim about its significance.

But their theory supports an ancient narrative, elaborated in Zecharia Sitchin series *Earth Chronicles,* and recorded on cuneiform tablets over 8,000 years ago, that there is a massive planet named Nibiru which orbits our sun every 10,000 years and its orbits could be destructive to life on Earth. On its last orbit, its gravitational pull dislodged a large sheet of ice, covering the continent of Antarctica, into the Indian Ocean which displacement accounted for the flooding referred to in the Bible. And according to Sumerians, this is the planet of our Gods, so called because of its inhabitant's superior technological skills. Further, according to Sitchin, it was a collision between a satellite of Planet Nibiru and Planet Tiamat, at the time located between Jupiter and Mars, which caused the formation of Earth in its present location and the smaller parts formed the asteroid belt between those two planets. Scientists are of the opinion that Earth did undergo a collision causing the formation of its moon, thus giving credence to the Tiamat scenario.

Monoliths and megaliths around the World, including well known ones such as the Pyramids & Sphinx of Giza, Angkor Wat, Gebeke Tepe, Stone Henge, and Machu Picchu, attest to their occupation of the Planet.

If the planet of our Gods is approaching, and it is affecting the orbit of Earth, can this account for the rapid change in climatic conditions being witnessed? And will this lead to the prophesy that when our Gods return, it will be the end of times? Food for thought.

Despairing Populations

As fact checked by Reuters, it was Danish politician Ida Auken, who wrote the prediction that by 2030 we will own nothing and be happy. She said it was not a "utopia or dream of the future" but "a scenario showing where we could be heading—for better and for worse."

VIII (H) – CHAPTER VII
(CHANGING COURSE)

Tethered Currency

During the 20th Century, the gold standard was in use from 1900 to early 1920s, late 1920s to 1932, and from 1944 to 1971. Wars have a tendency of upsetting the operation, smooth or otherwise, of asset-backed currencies. It was the first World War, 1914 to 1918, that brought an end to the gold specie standard in the United Kingdom and the rest of the British Empire. During the war, many countries suspended or abandoned the standard, due to the large deficits needed, and after, a run-on sterling caused Britain to impose exchange controls that fatally weakened the standard, though convertibility was not legally suspended. By 1927, many countries had returned to the standard, but this was quickly halted again by the effects of the Great Depression followed by World War II. Britain had adopted the gold bullion standard instead of the gold specie standard, ending the circulation of gold specie coins. But speculative attacks on the pound and runs on the banking system led Britain to abandon the gold standard, in addition to the need other countries had to stimulate their economies to reduce unemployment.

The gold standard returned in 1944 with the *Bretton Woods Agreement* with the *US* dollar representing gold valued at $35 an ounce. At the time, the *US* had about 80% of the world's gold stock and by tying its currency to gold, the dollar was gold transferrable in bullion among nations. This lasted until another war stepped in the way and the *US* funding of the Vietnam War by printing dollars, its transferability could not be sustained after Britain came calling in 1971. President Nixon ended international convertibility in August 1971, on a temporary basis, but that became permanent by October 1976.

Deflationary Policies & Transitory Income Support

The U.S. Treasury has developed the experience to effectively transfer funds to individuals and households from its 2020/2021 stimulus pandemic relief-programs. Transfers made were generally in the form of direct deposits into bank accounts. As deflationary policies reduce the income of individuals/households, government income support programs become essential. These would have to be targeted support programs to avoid defeating the purpose of reducing demands from the deflationary policies, i.e., lowering the cost-of-living. This becomes easier with the transition to a digital currency platform where incomes can be verified and payments directed to the intended, such as rent payments to landlords. And to ensure that those receiving income support have minimum discretionary income available.

Some economists are of the opinion that government support programs are best implemented through government tax credits. The term tax credit refers to government funds taxpayers can deduct directly from the taxes they owe and are granted to promote specific behaviors that benefit the economy and environment, such as the substitution of electric over combustion vehicles, or for subsidy-type programs. The use of tax credits should not be a problem in executing an income-support program providing the credits are refundable, i.e., that a taxpayer, regardless of income or tax liability, is entitled to the entire amount of the credit. So, if the refundable tax credit reduces the tax liability to below $0, the taxpayer is still due a refund.

Restrictions on Debt

Until 1917, Congress authorized increases in public debt but needed to provide more flexibility due to the funding of World War 1. That resulted in it placing a cap on this debt without having to devote attention to each and every bond issued. As limits are approached, the treasury would inform Congress, which would make amendments to ensure the U.S. would not default. According to the Department of Treasury, "since 1960, Congress has acted 78 separate times to permanently raise, temporarily extend, or revise the definition of the debt limit—49 times under Republican presidents and 29 times under Democratic presidents". However, during the 1995-1996 budget crisis, the U.S. Government did shutdown and the budget that year did not pass.

Over the last decade or so, Treasury informed Congress of several instances when the debt ceiling would have been breached and the U.S. Government came close to default but for some extraordinary measures by the Treasury, such as the suspension of investments in employee retirement programs. The potential defaults arise because there is no coordination between the approval of programs/projects and their funding. The problem occurs when costs are incurred but payment of them would have violated the cap on debt. The ceiling is thus a limit on the ability to pay obligations already incurred and represents a real potential for default.

The Treasury is of the opinion that failure to increase the debt limit would have dire consequences. It says "failing to increase the debt limit would have catastrophic economic consequences. It would cause the government to default on its legal obligations—an unprecedented event in American history. That would precipitate another financial crisis and threaten the jobs and savings of everyday Americans". During the financial crisis of 2011, when S&P issued the first ever downgrade in the federal government credit rating, this along with the debt ceiling debacle at that time, contributed to the Dow Jones Industrial Average falling nearly 2,000 points around mid-year, with one historical daily drop of 635 points.

The current ceiling in 2022 stands at about $31.4 trillion and should be exceeded by mid-year, 2023.

Reducing Income and Wealth Inequality

To fix economic inequality, this book recommends establishing an income relationship between the lowest and highest paid in society, and taxing income above that of the statutory highest paid at an exorbitant rate. These extra tax revenues will then be used as transfer payments to the lower paid by mitigating food, housing, healthcare, and education and training costs. The Peterson Institute for International Economics (PIIE) proposed a similar general approach along production stages of pre-production, production and post-production. Then combined in a matrix with bottom, medium and top earners, shown on the next page, laid out multi-faceted solutions to the problem (**Figure 34**).

	Pre-Production	*Production*	*Post-Production*
Bottom Earners	Expanded access to healthcare and education; Universal Basic Income	Minimum wage policies; job guarantees	Government transfers, including Earned Income Tax Credit; full-employment policies
Middle Earners	Public spending on higher education and training programs	"Good Jobs" policies; industrial relations and labor laws; sectoral wage boards; trade agreements; innovation policies	Social security nets; social insurance policies
Top Earners	Inheritance and estate taxes	Corporate regulations; antitrust laws	Wealth taxes

Figure 34

Source: Oliver Blanchard and Dani Rodrik, PIIE Blog Post, "We have the tools to reverse the rise in inequality"

Population Control

In 1952, India became the first country with a 5-year plan outlining its population control policies. Over time, and many 5-year plans later, it is still looking for a viable way to control its population. These plans addressed several approaches to population control, including forced sterilization, postponement of marriageable ages, availability of public birth-control services, reduction of infant mortality rates, consideration of coercive penalties that limit access to government jobs and subsidies, and programs that incentivize conformance. In 2021, the Population Control, Stabilization and Welfare Bill proposed incentivizing a family conforming to the Total Fertility Replacement Rate of 2 children with housing subsidies and soft loans, tax rebates, increased pensions, and free health care facilities. For those not conforming would be denied access to government social programs and jobs, and other restrictions. India's experience with population control demonstrates the resistance from social and cultural customs that other nations will face as they try to reduce world population, an essential objective.

IX

INDEX OF MAJOR CONCEPTS